South Oxhey Estate

Days of Wonder at the Dawn of Rock & Roll

PETE BOULTER

Contents

THE BARNES ESTATE

An old man killing chickens in the next-door garden. Released from his certain fingers they ran broken-necked, in circles, to death.

An old man handling an oar, three metres of Thames driftwood.

Mr. Agutter, the neighbour on the other side, handing me a box full of used dog track tickets.

My Grandfather, an old man living in the downstairs front room, solitary and one-legged, drinking jug beer from the Boileau arms, giving us coloured pencils, singly, on rare and grave days. My knowledge of his death, the voices of mourners.

'Looks better, younger, rosy, wax they use…'

I wanted to see him, but did not have the words. I was kept amused by strangers, who themselves took turns to view the body.

Over Hammersmith Bridge and along Lower Mall, upriver past the dreadful noise of the pump house.

Burying a saw from my toy woodwork set and being unable to find it again.

Patches on the wallpaper where furniture and the fireplace mirror had been, an empty house before the move.

Going with my mother to collect my sister, Jean, from the nearby school. A clear memory of rows of coat hooks and benches under them.

My father, home from work, taking a folded bus ticket from between his teeth, whistling the joyous dog running up Lonsdale Road to meet him.

A big house with a black stone cat fixed halfway up the wall.

A dead boy in King Street, Hammersmith, his chest caved under the double-decker's wheel.

A visit to the other house, the one we were going live in, and seeing the sad exchange family gathered around a fire with glass doors; the man showing me a mould for making lead soldiers.

That's all I remember of my birthplace and the first four years living at 2 Nowell Road, on a small council estate in Barnes, Surrey. I spent long pleasant days alone in the big garden; digging holes and peering through the chestnut paling fences. Coincidence has led me back to the area several times in recent years, and there is a sense of familiarity about the streets, but no feeling of regret at having moved away. The houses have weathered down now, and ivy covers much of the pebbledash, there are trees I do not remember from before, nor the constant roar of aircraft stacking over Heathrow.

My parents had lived in Fulham, then moved to Peabody Buildings in Lawrence Street, Chelsea, where my father's parents also lived. His father was the superintendent of the building. From there they moved to Lillian Road, Barnes, to be nearer my mother's parents, who were both in poor health. This was where my sister Jean was born on the third of January 1939. Then, after her own mother died, my mother moved again, with my father and my sister, a short distance to live with her father at Nowell Rod. I was born in the Nursing Home, further along the same road, on 9th January 1944.

My Uncle Fred, one of my mother's brothers, also lived at our house, and both he and my father were called up into the armed forces, and posted overseas. It was a difficult time for my mother, her father was ill, and there were air raids, and wartime shortages. At one stage, my mother was evacuated, and my sister and I went with her to Birmingham. We stayed there for six weeks, long enough for my sister to attend school. My mother, worried about her ailing father left behind, decided to return to London. Fortunately, my father's ship, a destroyer, was home for repairs at the time and he was given compassionate leave to visit us. We all left together on the train back to London.

Upon our return, Jean was found to have diphtheria, then my mother also showed symptoms. Both were admitted to the same hospital. My mother left hospital first, but my sister remained ill, and was in an oxygen tent for a while. When she finally did come home, Jean caught Scarlet Fever and returned to hospital. Having recovered from that, yet continuing to be unwell, Jean was found to have asthma, and was eventually sent to stay at two different convalescent homes. She would struggle with this asthma for many years ahead. I was too young to be aware of all these family problems then, of course, and it was only much later when I saw how serious Jean's chronic attacks were, and how quickly they could develop.

My father and my Uncle Fred, were both demobbed and returned from overseas to live at Nowell Road. This triggered a period of slow domestic recovery, overshadowed by a family tragedy. One my father's nephews, our cousin Tony, returning home after a visit to our house, fell from the Barnes towpath into the Thames, and was drowned. A passer-by dived in to save him but he also drowned, both caught and held in the powerful currents swirling around the bridge supports.

I do not know exactly why we left the Barnes estate, why my parents should have wished to leave a familiar environment for a largely unknown one. My father in particular, appears to have had little reason to make such a move. He had grown up, with his six siblings, in a block of flats in Lawrence Street, Chelsea, just behind the grand houses of Cheyne Walk and the Thames. A gas-lit building with both the cold water tap and the W.C. located outside the flat on the communal landing. The landings, stairs, and walkways, were of ironwork exposed to the elements.

He had been a stoker on a destroyer during the war, survivor of a German submarine attack and a direct hit from a Japanese kamikaze pilot. When he returned from the war, he went back to his previous job as a skilled coach painter, working for Mulliner Park Ward in Hythe Road Willesden, a company making custom bodies for Rolls Royce.

The Barnes house was a in a convenient location, an easy walk to Barnes Village and the Common, or across the bridge to Hammersmith, and not a great distance from my father's work place. He was near his friends and relatives, and the attractions of the Pier Hotel along the river and the Furnival Club on Lower Mall. I think he also frequented the Cross Keys in Lawrence Street. I can't see how he could have been attracted to life on a new housing estate in Hertfordshire.

It is likely that my mother had more cause to leave the area. The youngest daughter of the Pugsley family, she had spent a happy childhood with many sisters and brothers in a riverside house at 20 Lower Mall, Hammersmith. The house faced the river, which was just a few yards away, and the bridge was close by. In 1928, on the 7th of January, high spring tides flooded the house. My mother told me told the family were alerted to the rising water by one of her brothers, Bill, as he arrived home. As their possessions drifted away on the muddy flood tide, the family escaped from an upstairs window, in a boat. They were later rehoused on the Barnes Estate, across the river. Living in that house, now with her own family, and her parents both dead – perhaps my mother decided to make a fresh start elsewhere, and follow her eldest sister, Emmie, out of London to a huge council estate that was still being built in Hertfordshire.

Another reason for moving, possibly the most significant, was that a doctor had suggested that the family move away from the river, that it might help relieve Jean's asthma. The local council were informed and a house exchange was arranged with a family living in on the same estate as her sister.

THE SOUTH OXHEY ESTATE

We moved to South Oxhey in 1948, when I was four years old, it was still unfinished, a huge estate of new housing with a physical barrier on every side; fields, woods, a railway track and a golf course.

It was a project developed by the London County Council. The new council estate was built around the manor house, Oxhey Place, owned by the Blackwell family, of the Crosse and Blackwell company.

In the grounds of the house was a chapel built in 1612 that still exists. I can only remember two other original buildings, an old house near the road bridge over the railway in Little Oxhey Lane that became a public library, and a strange barnlike building by the Big Woods called Wooden Bygones and seemed to be a kind of rural museum. I was never inside it to check.

Nearby, there were two private estates. Oxhey Hall was mostly large semi-detached houses separated from us by the golf course. It was of little interest to us as there were no shops there. Across the railway line, however, at Carpenders Park, there was another private estate, and a parade of shops. The majority of the properties there were bungalows.

When we arrived the South Oxhey estate was only half completed. A square mile of mud, clay, cinders, chalk and building materials. I was not aware at the time that a mile away from South Oxhey, near Bushey Station, were places called Chalk Hill, Clay Hill, and Claybury.

A vast number of children of all ages roamed the unmade streets. The schools were overloaded. The first six months at school I was mornings only or afternoons only. I remember a day of labels around our necks, and playtime gangs and fighting. I cannot remember the names of any of the staff, but there were trees that produced crab apples and oak apples and shiny acorns.

WOODHALL LANE

Our house was in Woodhall Lane, in Tintown, an area of the estate that faced the railway track. The houses were prefabricated to some extent, with the upper half and roof seemingly made of corrugated iron. This was actually corrugated asbestos I believe. There were three bedrooms; one for my parents, one for my sister and me to share, and a tiny bedroom over the stairs for Uncle Fred. He was a man of intelligence and sensitivity and pride, [He sent his medals back] a sad, kind bachelor, a reader of books and a labourer in an iron foundry in Watford.

In front of the house was a very large oak tree encircled by a brick wall. Beyond the tree was a quiet roadway, a fence, then the pair of slow line tracks running from Watford to Broad Street and Euston. The Bakerloo Line trains also went out as far as Watford then, giving access to the West End and beyond. After these, inaccessible from the station, were the tracks for the fast main line trains leading to and from Euston, and the goods train tracks.

With the adults at work, we threw local clay at the trains, formed into rounded lumps and flung from whippy sticks. A little further up the road we could get through the fence and pick the small wild strawberries on the embankment, which ran gently down to the tracks. Later I was to cross the tracks with my sister. It seems incredible now, six years old, crossing six sets of tracks, two of them electrified.

'Don't step on that one, Peter,' said my sister.

And I remember racing up Woodhall Lane to see two dogs mating. Most of the local kids standing around, as the angry owners threw buckets of water over the dogs. We were amazed by the dog's persistence.

Brenda, the fat girl up the road, saved my life perhaps, certainly my future health. The doctor parked his car at the top of Woodhall Lane - a steep hill - and forgot to put the handbrake on. The car rolled gently backwards, gathered a fair amount of speed, mounted the pavement and came straight across the pavement and onto the green in front of the houses where we were hanging around in the Jolliffe's front garden. We were not alarmed as the car was going quite slowly now. It moved silently across the grass. Brenda pulled me away just before it hit the gatepost and snapped it in half, a hefty no nonsense council gatepost. We were all within a metre of the now stationary car, unhurt.

A big brown radiogram, mahogany veneer and dark Bakelite: leaning close to hear *Dick Barton Special Agent* and a Bruce Woodcock fight. It seems odd now that I can remember nothing else I heard on the radio in those early years, apart from the shipping forecast with its mysterious sea areas like Dogger, Heligoland, Rockall and Fastnet.

Dad, talking to me once, telling me about when he was a boy. How he used to sit in bed with a string tied around the bedposts for reins, whipping the air with a string on a stick, a thin leather end for a snapper. He also told me of catching free rides down the King's Road, out of sight on the backs of carts, and pedestrians calling out to the driver.

'Whip behind guv'nor!'

Because of this story, I made a whip with a lead-weighted sash cord. Mum, walking out of the kitchen and then crying out and holding her hands over her eyes. Dad awkwardly holding her. I remember her anger and his evasion of my punishment.

Sometimes he bought home a bag of sweets on his pay nights, half a pound of all different kinds. Two or three times he arrived home with Lyon's ice-cream, wrapped in layers of newspaper, kept cool between layers of dry ice that burned your fingers if you touched it.

Mum worked part-time, first at the Kodak Factory in Harrow, and then at Blyth & Platt Limited at Solar Works in Greatham Road, Bushey. This was a shoe polish factory. It was known locally as Cobra after a well-known polish manufactured there, and later referred to as Wren's after the company name changed to Meltonian Wren. After Mum left the polish factory, she took me back there to collect her wages. There had been a big flood in that area, where the River Colne crossed Water Lane, and we walked on a raised walkway with sandbags along the sides, surrounded by fields of water.

Uncle Fred had a black bike, and walked it home one day with a Stanley vice on the saddle. He kept apart from the family, reading and making things, not ever going out. He had made a big box that was kept under his bed to keep belongings in. He had an old cast-iron junction box, and I pestered him make it into a camera for me. I remember well that gentle smile and the way he turned the box in his hands, over and over, knowing it was impossible but not wanting to say it.

Saturday was Co-op van day. A large trailer parked on waste ground, the wheels removed, selling groceries cheaper than the travelling vans. I remember the bright red van and the queue, and playing with all the other children, often waiting two hours to be served.

I used to go with Jean over to the other side, over the green wooden railway bridge to the sweet shop. I can remember tearing out the coupons to give to the lady. Jean had met a girl who lived over there, she had been caught in a thunderstorm and the girl had asked her in. We went to visit her once. We did not go in, but stood in the porch as the girl showed us how she could skate in her socks on the polished woodblock floor. We left without having a go ourselves.

'Where's Jeep?' I asked once.

'Well,' said my mother, 'I'm afraid I've got bad news for you, Peter. Jeep died three weeks ago, during the night.'

Not having noticed our old cat was missing until that day, I could not really raise much enthusiasm for grief, and anyway, we managed to get a new one. Tibby was salvaged from the remnants of a litter that a local boy had been playing with. Most of the kittens were broken, my sister Jean managing to grab our healthy one just as he was being pushed through a letterbox. I called it Tiger and everybody else called it Tibby.

One day our dog Trixie was nose to nose in a quivering encounter with a large and ferocious dog from up the road. We were all afraid of this animal, and all the local kids were standing around saying that our dog would have its throat ripped out without a doubt. Trixie was saved by the spectacular intervention of the new cat, who sprang between the two and hooked a paw into the big dog's nose. It ran off howling, pouring blood. We followed the bloodstains on the pavement back to the owner's house, then drifted home gleefully.

In the house next door to us lived Mr. Mead. He was quiet and soft-spoken, a smiling, pleasant man with glasses, a club-footed hunchback with a funny moped. It had a motor that rubbed on the front tyre and he limped all over to one side when he pushed it up or down the ramp by their front steps. He had a large wife with a loud voice, a son called John, and a daughter called Sweetie. His wife would lean over the side gate and talk to my mother about operations.

Robert Hardy was big. He hit me on the leg with an ex-army folding spade. Two hours after the incident I emerged from our house and pushed him backwards off a high wall. I could have seriously injured him, and his parents had words with mine about the matter. Looking back, the episode appears to be a significant one, being possibly the first example of a tendency towards disproportionate reaction, often violent and carefully planned in advance.

The Jolliffe family lived up the hill. Famous rough kids they were out of our class in those days. We played with their father's two-edged Japanese sword and undressed in their shed. Best of all, we dug up their dog, dead for three months. The smell was a giveaway, and neighbours with angry faces made us bury it again.

We lived on the edge of the Chilterns where the chalk met London Clay and was turned up by the bulldozers. We played hopscotch in the street, using the great chunks of chalk that lay everywhere to draw the squares. The top square contained the word LONDON. It was not until I was in my mid-twenties that I discovered the top square was supposed to read HOME. Home in our game was always marked as London, a standard alteration throughout the estate.

Aunt Edie came to stay once. She worked in a Bayswater kitchen, living in. Her son Lennie lived with my Aunt Louie and Uncle George and her daughter stayed with her ex-husband. Jean and I really liked her. She was even pretty when asleep on Jean's bed in the afternoons. Once I piled an assortment of shoes around her head and she woke up laughing. I came home unexpectedly from school in the lunch hour to see her. I was supposed to stay for school dinner and stayed terrified in the locked bathroom as my mother arrived home and shouted for me to come out.

NORTHWICK ROAD

We moved to a bigger house, in the middle of the estate, with my new school just across the road. I remember the name of my teacher, Mrs. McNamee, the name of the school itself, Oxhey Wood Infants, and Oliver Hornby. He had two grass snakes in a shoebox and the teacher let him bring them to school.

'They're not poisonous,' he told me, 'but you better not touch 'em or they'll bite you.'

I was in the back garden of the new house, looking through the chain link fence, my face was hurting, I'd had three teeth out earlier in the day, and was remembering the smell of the gas mask, buying the comic outside the pub, and walking down the High Street with the clean rag pressed to my face. I was watching some boys playing rounders behind our garden, on the waste ground. Dusk. A warm summer's evening. Not knowing any of them. The sharp click of the bat. Dad out in the garden too, calling one of them over.

'Alright if my boy plays with you? We've only just moved in round here and he don't know anybody yet.'

'Yeah, alright, mister.'

And a big kid taking me over the fence from my father's arms. Nervous and excited, wanting to play, without really looking, I walked forward into the backswing. A bloody great pickaxe handle or copper stick smacked me in the face. No pain at first. Then pain. Lifted back over the fence. Dad swearing, carrying me, stumbling back to the house.

I had moved up into the juniors, to a young woman teacher who had bad eyes and had to wear dark glasses. I missed my infant teacher, Mrs. McNamee, and once stood sadly outside her bungalow over the other side of the railway, hoping she would appear and ask me in.

I read *Salar The Salmon* and *Bruno The Bear,* two books in an animal series in the classroom library corner. At home I worked through a huge pile of Uncle Fred's magazines, old copies of *Practical Householder* and *Practical Mechanics*. I remember plans and specifications for a blowlamp and a three-wheel car.

Uncle Fred lived downstairs now, in the front room of the new house. I did not see him so often and his door was usually closed.

I formed a secret society with Alan Morris and another boy. We held meetings under the carpet in the Morris house, with torches and green triangles painted on cardboard identity badges. The society folded as Mrs. Morris grew tired of our meetings.

Near the house, on the corner of our street, was another, much smaller area of waste ground. A few tree stumps that had been blown up with dynamite had been dumped there by contractors building a new secondary school behind our house. Two of the stumps lay close together and were each two metes high or more. Roofed over with branches and grass they became a shelter and a stage. A lot of the local children would gather there at weekends, including several older girls who organized plays. Younger children, myself included, were in great demand either as part of the complicated productions or as members of the audience.

Sometimes plays were advertised. The time of the performance was chalked up on a board on the corner of the waste ground. The girls would bring old sheets and blankets for stage curtains. The rest of the tree stumps formed a primitive arena. Costumes were usually limited to big hats, big dresses, high-heeled shoes and old handbags. Apart from the plays there also games of doctors and nurses and mothers and fathers but these were whispering occasions under the blanketed shelter and we were considered too young to participate.

With an older boy called Cookie, we lay behind a low ridge of excavated soil, a heavy smell of wet clay, waiting for the bottle of stolen petrol to explode when the rag fuse finally burned down. Also with Cookie we sat around a low fire watching a dead rat burning on the end of the wire.

Cathy Wells had a tortoise and its leg fell off. She kept both. It seems as if the leg had just rotted off and we were forever testing the other legs for similar signs of decay.

We heard that a local boy called Paul had been kicked in the stomach by Cookie and sure enough there was the trail of dark blood spots coughed along the street and up to his back gate. We all thought Paul would die, but he was only off school for a couple of days.

The new house was bigger than the old one in Tintown and had French windows leading out into the back garden. I was playing on my own out there one evening when Mum and Dad appeared and called me in. Dad put his arm around my shoulders.

'Would you like to have a baby brother or sister?'

'Don't want one.'

'Don't be silly, Peter,' said my mother, and I cried until they promised not to call a boy Stephen John and compromised with John Stephen.

After a few months, they passed me over the fence again, this time it was the side fence, to Mr. Rouse and his family, our neighbours, in exchange for a big China jug.

Later, I was called away from the happy Rouse kitchen, from the smoke and the playing cards and the six sons, taken home to see my new brother. I don't remember my mother's face, only her arms holding the wrinkled red baby. I was not afraid, nor excited, but awkward, as if not knowing what reaction was expected.

And then we had to leave, Jean and I, to spend that strange Christmas, that snowy Christmas of 1951, at the house in Home Farm Road, Hanwell, Middlesex. To Aunt Florrie and Uncle Harry, cousin Terry, cousin Barbara, and cousin Jack and his wife Eunice. A good place, busy, noisy, and cheerful. Not so much money then, but plenty of enthusiasm and joviality, a stripey-handled sheath knife and a big sloppy Labrador, snowmen and igloos, and a *Robin Hood* serial in the *Beano* delivered every Thursday. Uncle Harry used to sing "Ragtime Cowboy Joe" and Aunt Florrie was bossy but also laughed a lot.

I can't remember who opened the front door when we were eventually taken home in Uncle Harry's black Ford. We were taken into the front room, to unknown clutter, and scraps of torn-up paper on the linoleum. Uncle Fred no longer lived there. Nobody rose from the two off-white Rexine chairs close to the beige hearth, and the low pyramid of dull coke. Our mother seemed exhausted, empty, withdrawn, holding the baby, one stranger holding another. The man hunched forward towards the fire, staring blankly at, and turning with his red fingers, a yellow plastic windmill on a stick of split bamboo. My father, now an older, tired man, his awkward flat voice echoed from the other chair.

What happened here when we were away? Why should my Uncle Harry's voice, his jolly cheerio, sound so unbearably loud? I asked no questions then, nor later. We went up to bed. I was eight years old and cried in bed. Sobbed quietly so as not to wake my parents, chest jumping with despair and fear that had no concrete cause. And that downstairs room, that atmosphere of desolation, was to stay with me. I had no idea what had happened whilst my sister and I had been away, but something was lost then. I doubt if my parents saw any change in me, and things carried on much as before. In 2022, quite out of the blue, my sister Jean rang up and during the conversation she mentioned that we had been sent to stay with our cousins in Hanwell because my mother went into hospital with pneumonia after the birth of my brother, and he went into hospital with her. This would probably explain why things seemed so flat upon our return to the house. I can understand now why we were not told at the time.

I was absorbed back into the school and street life, and having a baby brother around the place was useful in that my mother had a lot less time to keep an eye on me. I enjoyed school and loved being out of the house playing with the other children. Children who had to be in early or go out with their parents were annoying. I wanted to be accepted by older children and I wanted a red-handled Swiss Army knife.

HAYLING ROAD

When I was nine we moved again, to a smaller, terraced, house. The rent was cheaper. I remember the van, and greasing the cat's paws with margarine. There were fewer children in the area but most of them were my age. The house was in Hayling Road, one of the two main roads on the estate, and the back garden overlooked paradise, a disused golf course with green fairways, sandy bunkers, ditches, and deep wooded dells. Almost directly behind the house was a newly built recreation ground with a green flat top roundabout, a witch's hat, swings and a horizontal, chainless swing boat.

There was also an abandoned orchard, with apple, damson and hazelnut trees, and a rubbish dump full of old bikes and prams collected by the tractor man. Not far away, there were the Big Woods, extending uphill towards Northwood, dark with trees and rhododendrons. At the bottom of the road was a fast-flowing stream with fat rats at dusk, and smaller wooded area that we called the Railway Woods, and a steep railway embankment with a cattle tunnel underneath, leading to a bigger wood, a cornfield, and Carpender's Park. A walk to the top of the abandoned golf course took us to an old mill house and the River Colne, flooded gravel pits and the private fishing signs. There were also a few half-sunk barges we liked to think were Viking longboats.

Things were difficult at home. My father had been off work for some time with mumps and a double rupture. The atmosphere at home could be nasty, and there was a long succession of bitter parental rows, usually at night when I was in bed. The people next door had real fights, screaming and ranting and throwing things, but our parents had low-level rows that went on and on, ending in silence. They would not speak to nor of each other for day's and eventually for weeks. Once I went downstairs.

'Please Mum can you stop it? I can't get to sleep.'

She became instantly enraged, grabbing me and dragging me to the foot of the stairs, both hands were around my throat. I was stunned by the unsuspected violence.

'Go back to bed, get back to bed or I'll kill you.'

Perhaps she lost control because she was ashamed, or because by appealing to her I suggested that she was the cause of the row. I don't know. I learned to keep my mouth shut. I hardly spoke to them anyway. My father was seldom around, and any talk with my mother ended in accusations of sarcasm. The only times she spoke at length was when I was sick and away from school, which was fairly often. I had recurrent bouts of tonsillitis and bronchitis. On such occasions my mother was wonderful, although with the years of worry and physical strain looking after her parents and my sister, she'd already done more than her fair share. She was pleasant and cheerful, reading to me and telling stories and fetching hot Ribena. I could not ever complain of physical neglect, even my father occasionally read to me, although I rarely saw him read anything otherwise. His hot drinks always arrived lukewarm, he was nervous and impatient when confronted by sickness and could never wait for the kettle to boil.

The stories that my mother told were of the old days when she belonged to a big happy family, a kind of London working-class *Little Women*. She would also tell me of how she would have left my father long ago if it were not for the children. Despite such talks I did not blame my father any more than my mother for the frequent lack of family joviality. My silent condemnation was applied equally to both.

I could however, escape. Eventually a new job kept my father occupied and the new baby kept my mother busy. My sister was usually out or hiding in her bedroom playing records. She was old enough for me to confide in but too old to play with. I could go out early and sneak back in late. All that was required was that I stated my destination and friends, and managed to run the odd errand to the shops. I was small and thin, but I was crafty, agile, and quite good at fighting, tree climbing, and roller skating. At home, trapped for odd hours or days by bad weather and other misfortunes, I sought refuge in books. I could get down on the floor with a book and be shut off completely from the tensions on the upper levels. My mother read as well, and I always thought that my father found it annoying, anti-social perhaps, and that he was left out.

The Northwick Road Christmas had seen the end of Uncle Fred as a family fixture, he had left behind his heavier possessions, the large metal-working vice, the toolbox, and the books. Looking back, I can't be sure if they were all his books or the Pugsley family books. Most were from the *Everyman Classics* series, plus a great many engineering and technical books. My favourites were *Wuthering Heights*, *Lorna Doone*, *Le Morte D'Arthur*, *Frankenstein* and the poems of Alfred Lord Tennyson. On windy days over the golf course I was Heathcliff, forever vowing silent vengeance on all manner of people.

A large suitcase full of books was passed down to me from Lenny Dewsall, Aunt Edie's son, who lived with my Aunt Louie and Uncle George. There were Enid Blyton and *Just William* books, animal stories, Westerns, and adventure stories.

Les Hall lived next door with his parents, he'd just completed his National Service in Germany and his mother let me salvage a stack of books and magazines destined for the bonfire. These were really exciting. American adult books and magazines full of sex and sadism, war stories, and true murder cases. I read them in the rotting shed at the end of our garden, with a light from a Woolworth's paraffin lamp and a spyhole in the wall to check if anybody was coming.

Oxhey Wood School was only half a mile from our new house, but served an entirely different catchment area. I was in the top stream of a school with a good reputation, my street friends were mostly in the lower streams of a local school with a bad reputation. I was in an awkward position. I could not join in the school talk with the local gang, and was stuck with being a bit of an outsider. My experiences at school were not communicated to anybody at home, and each day I returned to the school with the events of the previous day still burning brightly, not having been modified by repetition or discussion. My attention level in class was not good, my main concern being the silent and frantic mental revision of previous lessons or experiences. It was a hopeless task, my filtering of earlier information constantly interrupted by the current demands of the teacher or the other children.

I remember writing a short poem for a girl in my class. She and her family moved to Australia and we all wrote in her goodbye notebook. Thoughts of the distance involved, and of never seeing her again, were cause for private concern in quiet moments.

I loved playtimes. From a quiet and restricting classroom we ran into the noisy playground and the big games field behind. Back to our rules, we sang "Ring Rang Roo" and "Good morning Mr. Murphy." These songs had lots of swearing and sexual references. Barry Adinall taught us the songs and could usually explain the more obscure lyrics.

We flicked cigarette cards up against the dustbin shed wall. The one that landed closest to the wall was the winner, and whoever threw it kept all the other cards. The rough-edged cards from Turf cigarette packets were not allowed. I managed to win over three hundred cards, including a set of famous cricketers.

We played marbles. The rules for the way we played were simple. We took it in turns to start the game by throwing a marble a few metres away on the tarmac. Then whoever else was playing tried to roll or throw their marble to hit it, if successful they then owned the struck marble. The use of ball bearings as marbles was hotly contested, and the children would often object to their use. Much heavier, they could easily chip or smash the coloured glass marbles.

Mostly, however, we played Kingy. You simply threw a tennis ball at one of the gang and if it hit them, they were it, the object of jeering derision until they managed to hit somebody else. The excitement of the game was that you were allowed to run wherever you liked, and throw the ball as hard as you liked and from as close or far away as you wished. Having the skill and speed and aggression required I was a Kingy star. The dozy kids always ran jerkily and needed their arms to keep balance, so leaving their faces exposed.

I found Vivian Henderson fascinating. There was nothing you could actually pin down as being wrong with her, and she was not disliked by the other children, but she would sometimes look slowly and deliberately at you, without speaking, as a teacher or another adult might do, looking for signs of guilt or dishonesty. As a child, I found this slightly intimidating. Much taller than I was, we played kiss chase over the golf course. I remember us ending up on the edge of a steep bank, and my clumsy attempt to embrace her, hopefully prior to the actual kissing. Fighting silently and desperately for a toehold in the slippery grass, and failing completely, we ended up sliding down the bank in a tangle. We didn't laugh, it was suddenly a serious and embarrassing business. At my instigation, we even had a song, *The Isle of Capri*. Five years later, at fifteen, I was to whistle half a verse and Vivian, fifty yards ahead, was to finish it.

Home time was always a time of confusion. To leave school and walk straight home, using the back entrance, was to walk alone past the jovial groups returning from the school near where I now lived, and to leave with most of my classmates, from the front entrance, meant walking in the wrong direction for some way, and then going home via the new shopping centre opposite the station. Either way I lost, either walking with children who were planning on meeting up again later, or getting stared at and into scraps with local schoolchildren simply because I was alone and walking against the stream. Mostly, my choice relied upon my mood. If I was happy I would use the long way home, if I unhappy I would snarl along the short route regardless.

There was a patch of woodland near the front of my school, and one afternoon I saw a crowd of boys gathered beneath a high elm tree. A dray at the top had been smashed to pieces by stones and the family of four squirrels were rushing about the upper levels. Unable to get down past the crowd they were also unable to make the huge leap needed to reach the safety of the next tree and then to the woods beyond. Two of the boys had .177 calibre air rifles, and at that that range could hardly miss. The two adults and the two youngsters jerked every time they were hit but the guns lacked the power to bring them down. I suppose they would've survived, dusk and teatime would have saved them if the new boy had not arrived. A quiet kid with a home-made hawthorn bow. His first attempt and an adult came down, a grey bundle with big eyes frantically trying to co-ordinate and jump and run, the arrow through its stomach.

'Bloody old tree rat!'

The squirrel was clumsily kicked, and smashed against the tree and generally battered to death, and the tail half cut and half torn off for the two shillings bounty. I felt little distress. Like the rest I was jealous of the silent stranger with the bow. He and others like him added threat and menace to the simple nuisance category into which adults placed us.

Away from school I played with the local children, a small gang that was to increase in size as we grew older and the street boundaries became less important. Stefan Miller was my age, a stocky black-haired Roman Catholic. Quick thinking and crafty, he was a good fighter and a liar. His brother Adrian was two years older and was very quiet and well spoken. Although he was strong and capable he lacked enthusiasm and spent much of his time worrying about Stefan. Mickey Goldsmith was also my age, a big slow-moving boy who was valued for his constant availability and steady good humour. Dick Herbert was a year younger, and like Micky he was readily available. Unlike me he was very energetic and daring, prepared to take a chance with the older kids in risky situations. Alan and Richard Fordham were, like the Millers, my age and two years older respectively. Also like the Millers the older brother was very much the quieter of the pair. Practical and reliable, their loyalty towards the group provided much of its stability, and their hefty build much of its security.

We made incredibly noisy trolleys from old scaffolding planks and ball bearing wheels. Old pram wheels were faster but were much harder to fix and did not sound so good. We played a form of hockey on roller skates, using golf balls and walking sticks, forever attempting the 'Double Eagle.' This was a specialist manoeuvre that none of us ever did manage to execute without falling over, even with the more expensive rubber-wheeled skates.

I made large and noisy whips, five metres of sash cord with a thin cracker slip on the end and a short heavy handle. The effort required to crack the thing was tremendous, but well worth it; the sound would echo across the golf course and around the nearby dell, as loud as a car backfire or banger. Then we all made even longer whips, taking it in turns to run along the edge of the dell whilst the others tried to encircle your legs and pull you over.

We roamed around the woods and golf course, building dams across the streams and making platform camps in trees. We dug underground camps in the golf course bunkers and roofed them over with sticks and leaves and a thin layer of sand on top to hide them. The same principle was used later to dig mantraps in the dell, half a metre deep pits in the soft leaf mould, covered with thin dry twigs and leaves and a thin covering of leaf mould, and the area carefully brushed with more twigs to hide the signs.

Many hours were spent in crawling silently through bushes to see who could get the closest to those courting couples that had carelessly strayed into our patch. We found used condoms we threw onto family doorsteps or hung on family gates, or threw them at each other with awful grimaces and mock vomiting.

On Saturday mornings we went to one of the cinemas in Watford, buying stale buns on the way home. I remember locking the door of a crowded dry cleaner's shop in the High Street. The shop door had a long outside bolt that could be padlocked when the shop was shut. The bolt was pulled up and turned in its housing to hold it in place. I only had to release it to lock the door. The customers were not shut in for long. From a distance, on the other side of the high street, we watched them tap on the window for a passing shopper to pull up the bolt. Strangely enough, they left it like that, perhaps I was the only person stupid enough to want to do it.

Three times a year a fairground was erected on the golf course, almost behind our house. From the arrival of the first trailer we would hang around the site, watching men put up the rides and stalls, and waiting for them to chalk up 'Open tonight at 7pm' on the sign in Hayling Road. In full swing the fairground generators chattered and hummed, the rides rattled on their metal tracks and the huge loudspeakers blasted out the latest sounds, crashing through the trees to where I lay, after my eight o'clock bedtime, in the back bedroom twilight.

The fairground kids were rough and exciting, but generally stayed away from us. The casual labour force was always attractive, but although more approachable, the men were really too old to give us much time. On Sundays and rainy days [which caused deep mud problems on the soft ground] when the fair was closed, we would sprawl around on the steps of the rides, cursing and spitting and waiting for something to happen. Nobody ever wanted to leave, kids from all over the estate would arrive, and if you went home you would almost certainly miss a good argument or a fight.

I went over to the railway tunnel with Mick Goldsmith and Norman Reeves, and a small whip made with Meccano and plaited leather shoelaces. From the tunnel entrance it was possible to climb up the embankment and reach the tracks, and Mick and I laid halfpennies on the goods line rails and waited to see them flattened. Norman was scared and would only go halfway up the embankment. We had been there a good half hour without a train arriving, so we decided to climb down again. We were nearly down when we saw a man waiting below, very smart in a fawn raincoat, collar and tie and shiny shoes.

'Right, you boys, I've caught you,' he said. 'No good trying to run off, I know where you live.'

And we just stood there, saying nothing. We were worried but there was nothing to say. The man sounded angry but had a peculiar sort of smile on his face.

'Trespassing on railway property,' he continued. 'I'm a railway detective and you'll get a summons for this.'

The threat of a summons did it for Norman, he started crying and groveling immediately. He kept saying how sorry he was, and how he would never do it again and the man kept right on smiling for a while, and then he came up with an offer.

'Well, you've got a choice. Either you can come with me now and be punished, or wait until the police come round your houses with a summons.'

So off we all went to be punished. Norman went ahead with the man and Mick and I tagged along behind. Mick and I did not want to be punished.

'He ain't no railway copper,' whispered Mick. 'I've seen him before, I think he lives in Birkdale Gardens.'

''Slow down a bit then, Mick, we'll drop back a bit further and then run for it.'

And I fell back slightly, whipping branches and kicking up leaves. The man was no longer concerned with us, he had stopped looking back and was nearly into the thicker part of the woods. He had an arm around Norman's shoulders and was talking to him.

'All right, Mick,' I muttered.

And we were away, running as fast as we could, over the little bridge and up through the thinning trees, stopping only when we reached the top of the bank on the edge of the woods. He could see us but had no chance of catching us. There was a busy road just a little further back behind us, and the golf course beyond that, full of people as it always was on Sunday mornings. We kept parallel with them for a while, creeping along the top of the bank in the bushes and long grass, the stream directly below and between us. They were on the opposite bank, and when they moved away, to go deeper into the woods, we gave up and went home.

Back at school after the holidays, Norman did not appear to blame me for abandoning him. The man had made him drop his trousers and bend over but had only smacked him a few times and then let him go. At least that's what Norman said. He had not told anybody, of course, and neither had we. We took the eleven-plus examination shortly after this episode, and then Norman and his family moved away. I promised to go and see him but never got around to it.

It was decided that I had to have my tonsils out, and I was taken to Bushey Cottage Hospital. It was bad experience. Too young to be in the men's ward, I was placed in a room with one seven year-old, two five year-olds, and three babies in cots. Only the babies were allowed visitors. I read *Two Years Before the Mast* by Richard Dana before the operation and a Western story magazine afterwards, having taken them both in myself. The last four days I had absolutely nothing to do except draw, there were no suitable toys or books. Mum sent in some grapes but they were shared among the wards and I received only two of them. After the operation I had hallucinations. Having had them before with tonsillitis, I knew what was happening, but it was still frightening. I told the night nurse.

'Stop fussing' she said. "Go to sleep now.'

And the weights were crushing my chest, giant coins were forcing the air from my lungs, my fingers were about to explode. I called her again.

'Please nurse I'm still having hallucinations.'

'Be quiet. You don't know what you're talking about boy. Shut up and go to sleep.'

And I cried them in anger and in helplessness. Hot and cold, heavy and light, head booming and spinning, chaos every time I closed my eyes. She came back.

'Now will you be quiet boy! Think yourself lucky, if you were twelve you'd be in the men's ward. You're too old for tears.'

And she marched off again, shoes squeaking on the shiny floor. Wishing I was in the men's ward, I stayed awake most of the night until my temperature dropped and I could close my eyes without fear.

BUSHEY GRAMMAR SCHOOL

'What are your hobbies?' asked Mr. O'Connor, the headmaster.

'Skates,' replied Tony Holmes, bright-eyed dynamo of Oxhey Wood Junior School.

'What troop are you in?' asked Mr. O'Connor.

And Tony Holmes was puzzled by this, but felt he'd better say something. They were waiting for him to continue.

'Oh, well, I...you know Sir, round the streets and that. Round Woodhall and Kilmarnock with my mates.'

Another pause, this time broken by the white-haired deputy.

'What can you tell us about Lord Baden- Powell?' It was an abrupt demand, and showed obvious annoyance.

'Sorry Sir, I've never heard of him,' said Tony.

And so Tony Holmes failed his eleven-plus interview. We knew him as a bright kid in our class, famous for his energy and humour, and because he claimed his mother would hit him with a cricket bat at the slightest provocation.

The next week it was my turn to find myself waiting in the long corridor, sitting underneath the sports trophy cabinet. I was the last one to be called into the study.

'Boulter, eh? There must be some mistake here. The interviews were supposed to be in alphabetical order. Why are you last?'

'Well sir, my first choice was Watford Grammar, but I changed my mind at the last moment because I found out it was a single sex school and I am used to a mixed school.'

This was a carefully rehearsed lie. I had discovered that most of my friends had chosen Bushey Grammar, and that the Watford Grammar interview would involve a mental arithmetic test.

'Hmm, I see. What are your hobbies?' Asked Mr. O'Connor, turning back from the sunny window view.

'Reading sir, especially animal stories.'

'Can you name a few books that you have read recently?'

'Yes Sir, *Black Beauty*, *Indian Paint*, and *The Call of the Wild.*'

'Have you read *Tarka the Otter*?'

'No Sir. Who was it written by Sir?'

And that was it, exactly the right thing to say. The rest of the brief interview was taken up by the headmaster relating the story and qualities founded in *Tarka the Otter* by Henry Williamson. I had no intention of being creepy, I was genuinely excited by his reference and had located and read the book myself within a few weeks.

Having passed the interview, it was necessary to attend the school with my parents on what was termed the Preliminary Visit. After a guided tour around the school and grounds, the parents were all herded into the main hall to be talked at, and the children were left with their assigned form teachers. I was immediately attracted to my form teacher, his name was Mr.

Pine, and he appeared to be kind and enthusiastic man, ready both to listen and to explain. He showed us balsa wood aeroplanes in his untidy classroom and copies of *Eagle* and *Girl* comics that he had delivered every week. He wore fawn cavalry twill trousers, a bright green shirt and a bright red knitted tie. He did not wear a jacket, had funny spiky hair and a red face. He kept on laughing and rushing about. I came away really excited, at the thought of being taught by an obviously cheerful eccentric in a room full of books, comics, and model aeroplanes.

When the parents were finally released from the main hall, I discovered that mine had somehow become involved with Robert Hine's parents, and that they were to accompany us on the long walk back to Bushey Station. I had already been stuck with the son earlier, as we had been placed in the same class, but had no desire to extend the experience. Robert Hine was different, no doubt about it. At Oxhey Wood he ate with his fingers and was generally regarded as odd. He and his younger brother had to be in bed by six o'clock, even in Summer, and for Christmas and birthdays received bibles and history books instead of real presents. His mother was an Austrian Jew, one of a family much depleted by Nazi endeavour, and the father was an ex-schoolteacher and soldier, now a local government clerk. On that walk to the station they were busy alarming my parents as to the problems we would encounter in the new school, of going from top of the year in a small school, to youngest and newest in a very large school. I was not concerned however, there were no problems, I had met the form teacher and he seemed all right.

The junior school experience was soon completed. A few days of quizzes and charades, goodbyes and autographed books, before starting the long summer holidays. My sister Jean had left Hampden Secondary Modern and now worked in a dress shop in Watford High Street, Dad was a painter at Scammell Lorries in Tolpit's Lane, West Watford, Mum was forty-one years old and brother John was three. We all went to a caravan near Clacton and stayed there for a week. There are photographs of us on the caravan steps, on the beach, and on the pier. There is a photograph of us all [apart from Dad who took the picture] standing under the Happy Valley Caravan Park entrance sign.

When we arrived home from the holiday I discovered that Stefan and Adrian Miller had moved away. Their parents had been trying to arrange an exchange for some time, trying to move back into London, and had finally managed it whilst I was away on holiday. It was a gloomy time for a few weeks afterwards, not only had they gone without goodbyes, but the new family and their house had only very young children.

The gang was now in need of new members and reluctantly we began to tolerate the presence of Jerry Price. Pricey had always been around, he only lived a few doors down from the Fordham brothers, but to us he seemed a bit odd He had been seen on several occasions in the First Dell, swooping up and down the bank wearing a Batman cloak and mask, on his own. He was a year older than I was, and went to Hampden Secondary School. A tall, good looking, and moody boy with doting parents, he was always clean and tidy and disliked the rough stuff.

One interesting thing about Pricey, was his dog. He made his parents get one because the Fordhams had a small intelligent mongrel called Bob. Nothing was too good for Pricey, so his parents paid out for a pedigree black Labrador. The dog was initially a disappointment. Whereas the Fordham's mongrel could do all manner of tricks on command, Pricey's Labrador could not even walk straight. It walked and ran slightly sideways and would fall over if running downhill. It made Pricey almost cry with rage. The dog proved to have one talent however, that did much to restore Pricey's self-respect. We had all wandered over to the lakes one day, to the sunken barges and the private fishing. Neither of the dogs had ever seen a large expanse of water before, and neither appeared very interested. Alan Fordham, man of action, threw Bob in. After two or three minutes he had to jump in after it, otherwise it would've drowned. We were shocked, and stood around the trembling dog in dismay, having believed that swimming was an inborn ability in dogs. A duck emerged from a patch of weeds and began to tread water and flap, prior to take off. Suddenly Pricey's dog wobbled to the edge of the bank and jumped straight in. It was a truly amazing sight, the stupid animal was faster in the water than it was on land! Not only could it swim in a straight line at high-speed, but it could actually show aggression, and very nearly caught the duck. After that display, and some flashy stick fetching from the water later, Pricey always wanted to go back over the lakes, but the Fordhams never fancied it.

Down to the bus stop at the bottom of Hayling Road, full of tea and hot Weetabix. I had a big blazer and long shorts, a canvas briefcase with brown plastic piping and a real leather strap. Getting off the bus at Bushey Arches and then waiting by the flint wall for another bus to take me to Bushey Grammar School and secondary education.

The beautiful building. A pitched red roof on light sand-faced brickwork, the school was built around a courtyard and a central assembly hall. Six years old and fronting onto farmland, with no houses to be seen beyond the porter's lodge, not even in winter. An art room, laboratories, and workshops. A separate dining hall and a huge library with a wrought iron balcony facing across Aldenham Road to the fields beyond. A small gym, four football pitches and a running track. The prefects had red piping on their blue blazers and most of the staff wore black gowns.

There were over a hundred children in the first year and I was the joint fastest rope climber of them all. I also made the school football team for three or four matches, but it soon became too cold and lonely for a small and skinny outside right. Many of the children came from South Oxhey Estate, and were already known to me. I also made friends with two boys in my class, Frank McGrory and Peter Naylor. McGrory was short and tough, a nonsmiling boy from central Watford: whereas Naylor was tall and well mannered, a smiling and handsome charmer even then. We applied ourselves to school work with varying degrees of success. McGrory was very capable indeed, his classroom manner was abrupt and his work untidy, but he excelled at mathematics and history and average in everything else. I was good at English and thought I was average in everything else, but my approach to work was impractical, I'd spend ages adding colour to maps, writing neatly, and careful underlining instead of getting things done quickly. Naylor seemed to be half asleep during classes but he was very popular with the girls.

Anthea Beardmore and Sylvine Woodrow both lived in a desirable residential area of Bushey. They both lived in houses next to a large park, the King George Recreation Ground, known for its swimming pool, and annual horticultural show. Sylvine Woodrow had a deep voice. She was half French and very small, extremely clever, and popular with both staff and pupils.

Anthea Beardmore was also very small, with black hair and big shiny eyes, and confidence in that slow smile. But mainly it was her voice that destroyed me. Her calm crystal diction, a voice to go with posh teas in summer gardens. I could not stop thinking about her. I kept a diary of events. AB smiled at me today. Asked AB to meet me after school. No luck.

I even thought a lot about her father, who wrote novels and a children's comic serial called *Belle of the Ballet*. I daydreamed about meeting him, and telling him I wanted to be a writer. I never did get to meet the man, however, and the daughter also remained almost a stranger. I had no chance of course, she simply could not understand what I was saying most of the time, and my mumbling snarl worsened with the embarrassment of not being understood. And there were other problems. Her humour was slow and childish compared to my own fast cruelty and cynicism. Her physical appearance was always so neat and tidy – always a sparkling cleanliness about those pleasing features. My own appearance was not so attractive. A yellowish complexion beneath the spots and grime, permanently dirty hands and chewed fingernails, and sweaty palms that left damp prints on books and tables. Possibly, much of my oily appearance was due to the daily application of the petroleum jelly I used to stick my curly hair down with. There was also Brylcreem, and another greenish hair product we got from Woolworths that came in an oval tin and had a faint scent of lavender.

No matter, I kept on trying to overcome these difficulties. I sent Christmas, Easter, birthday, and Valentine cards for three years or more, without acknowledgement, signing them with a matchstick figure borrowed from the novels by Leslie Charteris. I danced with her once in the rainy day school hall, pulling her too close and treading on her toes. I cycled alone to her Road, wheeling up and down outside – frightened to knock – hoping she might appear, and once sat with her on a school film trip. I put my arm around her in the friendly dark and kissed her.

'Anthea,' I said, 'Do you want a Spangle?'

'No thank you.'

Too late, I had already unwrapped one and put it into my mouth, a mouth too dry to dissolve it. I sat for twenty minutes in that cinema silence, frightened to move my teeth in case I crunched the boiled sweet. And then sat for a further hour and ten minutes, I could think of nothing to whisper and my arm was completely numb.

Another failure came later at an arranged meeting place, on the fresh mown green of King George's Recreation Ground. She had had agreed to meet me and had turned up with the family dog. A good sunny day and the grass dry enough to sit on. I had my bike, my green Lenton Special, and a pair of new grey Hong Kong jeans. I was astounded, she talked gaily for half an hour or more, of her family and herself, completely at ease. I had cycled a few miles to get there, but found myself with nothing to say, quite unable to simply talk easily with a classmate, unable to respond to that happy stream of eloquence. I finally mumbled and stumbled away with the Lenton Special.

Peter Naylor began to go to Sylvine Woodrow's house at weekends, to play tennis with her on the court in her back garden. He also talked easily with Anthea Beardmore. I could not accept this, he was getting too close. On some dreamed up pretext I challenged him to a fight in School Lane. I had only hit him a few times before he lay on the road, crying at first and then screaming.

'I'm blind, he's blinded me, I can't see!'

He was bluffing, naturally, but it worked for him. I was prevented from really sorting him out by the worried spectators, who held some obscure views about conduct in such matters. They seemed to think that fighting was somehow linked to honour, and that honour was satisfied once the opponent appeared beaten. They did not see that fighting could be enjoyed for its own sake, and that the primary aim was to cause pain and damage.

Towards the end of the first year my earlier enthusiasm for the school began to fade. I do not know what to say or how to act with the people that interested me. It was a confusing period. I was used to getting on well with most people back on the estate, yet was faced with continued rejection by the people at school that mattered to me. Even more annoying was that many of the other children on my estate seemed quite able to bridge the cultural gaps I struggled with.

I went to a school that was some miles from the two secondary schools on my estate, and was leaving home earlier and returning later than my local friends. I had to wear the hated school uniform and was labelled a 'Grammar Grub' without having any protective sense of superiority. Having failed completely to adapt, to make the best of my opportunity to do well at Bushey Grammar, I turned to the local streets for comfort.

The gang now had two new regular members. Mick Goldsmith, Pricey, and the Fordhams all went to Hampden Secondary Modern, and they had pulled in two of their schoolmates who happened to live nearby. They were both needed. Louis Letticer took over as chief fool from Dick Herbert, who was now as confident as the best of us, and Taff Evans, who showed us just how easy it was to get off with girls if you had a big smile and were very direct in your approach. We began to hang around the shopping centre in the evenings, and to walk around the estate looking for girls and anything else interesting.

Once we all went up to London on cheap off-peak tickets, to Soho. In those pre Wolfenden Report days, the girls were lined up all along Old Compton Street. Fantastic women, fur coats and high silver and gold shoes. And thin chains around their ankles, and some with small dogs too. Such beautiful women to us, seemingly cool, arrogant, hands-on hips against the wall, so lazily available. We could hardly believe it, we walked up and down the street with wild faces, wishing we were older and richer.

Jim Ward was Jean's latest boyfriend. He was thinner and slightly spotty then, but wore good tapered trousers and narrow ties. He was waiting to be called up for National Service. Jean brought him home a few times. Sometimes she would take me to Bill Taylor's cafe on the estate, with her friends, making one cup of tea last an hour.

'Don't drink it so fast Pete.'

Jean also gave me money for the jukebox. To feed in the coins and select "Heartbreak Hotel" from the list.

And it was absolutely the real thing thudding out of the Bal-Ami. Jean knew it and I knew it. I saw the Teds nodding in time and dangerous agreement. Elvis Presley, the young king – slicing through the steamy café with a screaming prophecy of the times to come.

It became necessary that I learned to swim before Mrs. Juba drowned me. A big woman Mrs. Juba, a swimming instructress who inspired no confidence. Told to glide across the baths it was my friend John Kavanagh who saved me, lifted me off the bottom eventually. She had not even noticed that I'd gone down to the bottom and stayed there. So, I went with Clarkey, another non-swimmer and fellow sufferer, to the Grand Union Canal at Croxley Moor. I had a sort of rubber inner tube thing with two straps I'd picked up from an army surplus shop. I had a plan. With the buoyancy aid inflated and strapped around my chest, I lowered myself into the canal at the bank and dog paddled along, really close to the edge, with Clarkey walking bent over on the bank above me ready to grab me if I needed help. Then I climbed out and Clarkey put the tube thing around him and he got in the water and paddled back to the starting point again with me walking close to the edge this time. Every time he got out I would let a little air out of the tube, get in the water and proceed as before. By the end of a long afternoon we could both swim ten yards, first with the tube fully inflated and then finally without using it at all. We spent the following morning at Watford Public Baths, encouraging each other to swim underwater, to seal dive, and even to dive clumsily head first into the water. It was more like falling headlong into the water with a desperate scramble to get upright again, but we felt a lot more comfortable in the water by then. At the next session with Mrs. Juba we both marched up to join the swimmers only group. She did not notice of course, or probably thought she had taught us.

Cahill was Irish. He was also very large and unpopular. He was a strange, awkward kid with a very rough background we assumed, and people generally kept away from him and avoided any confrontations. He spat at me one day and I immediately lashed out. It was a mistake. By the time the bell went and he had gone in, I had already stopped a number of good punches with my face. I should not have been upset, I was used to fighting and had been roughed up many times, but after he went in I cried in frustration, and then cried again at the shame of crying after a fight. This self-disgust was not considered to be important by the crowd, however, and for once the peculiar school codes worked in my favour. I was surprised to find that I had actually gained some prestige by fighting Cahill, and that he became even more disliked, was labelled a coward and a bully. I knew he was neither, like me he was just a kid whose background gave him problems at school, but whose size gave him a weight advantage in solving those problems.

Gene Vincent entered my world, black leathers and a leg-iron on a smashed leg, and "Be-bop-a-Lula" a medium paced Rock 'n' Roll song, sung so urgently. A breathless, boasting, sexy, song.

I was forever waving an ex-army jackknife around at school, and playing splits with McGrory, who had a single bladed ex-army clasp knife. He eventually threatened a girl at school with it. She remained calm, did not take him seriously enough, so he punched her lightly on the arm. Having been nearby, having been seen with a knife, I was judged to be guilty also. We were seen by our kindly form master, Mr. Pine and completely stunned by his reaction, so embarrassed to be present at his crack-up. He took us outside the classroom and made us stand against the corridor wall whilst he lectured us. He stayed there for ten minutes, white-faced and raving, and we saw him for a sad man, spluttering out his impotent rage so close to real despair. It was finished for us afterwards – we were nowhere with Pine for the rest of our schooldays, he would not speak to us if he could possibly avoid it. We had said nothing and remained unafraid. He did not even confiscate the knives.

'You will get nowhere in this life. You are both despicable cowards. You are rotten to the core. Rotten, simply rotten. Rotters, a pair of rotters.'

Streaming began in the second year and I was put into the Y Form. McGrory went up into the X Form and Naylor down into the Z. A few teachers asked my mother what had gone wrong.

'Peter should have been in the X Form. Hopefully he can settle down to work and go up next year.'

I have no idea if anybody ever did move up, but for me it could not be done. I was disappointed to be separated from some friends, and initially thought I would be able to make an effort, but that intention quickly fell away. I was to spend the next two and a half years coasting in the Y stream, sitting by windows watching the lorries roll past on their way to the Watford By-Pass.

Anthea Beardmore and Vivian Henderson were in the middle stream with me, and Mavis Elliott also. I really admired Mavis, she was very tough and almost an orphan. Her grandfather had fallen under a steamroller and had been buried in a sack, her mother was dead, and her father had put her in the care of the Royal Caledonian School. Mavis lived exactly next door to Bushey Grammar, in the horrific 'Cally,' a monstrous redbrick institution that looked like a prison or lunatic asylum. We could only meet at school. She was allowed out for two hours on Sunday afternoons but only to join the grim grey crocodile that marched up Aldenham Road and back.

Mr. Schapiro was our French teacher. He was French or Belgian, a very short, strange man, who generally seemed to be in a smouldering rage. He contacted the Cally administrative board for permission to take Mavis to a tea room in Watford at weekends. The permission was granted and she had little choice but to go. Mavis despised him as much as we all did. She would flick her fountain pen at his robe as he went past us, prowling around the aisles. We could see the ink flying.

A bonfire night to remember back on the estate. The older kids had collected lots of wood and any other combustible material they could find, and built an enormous fire on the ex-golf course, near a disused bunker, right behind our back fence. Too young again, I was called in at nine o'clock and had to watch from the back porch. A gang of older estate heroes, Snooky Webster and Eric Gough amongst them, were singing around the fire, "Giddy Up A Ding Dong" by Freddie Bell And The Bellboys.

I remember the dark November night behind the fire, crackling wood, and leaping flames, and faces picked out by the dancing firelight. Then they sang the Presley B-Side "Don't Be Cruel," Fats Domino's "Blueberry Hill," and Lonnie Donegan's "Don't You Rock Me Daddy-O" and "Lost John."

I spent a Sunday morning with Dick Herbert, ducking down behind the window ledge in the abandoned Crosse and Blackwell mansion, prizing a small amount of lead sheeting from the roof valley outside. We took it on a trolley to the George Ausden scrapyard in Watford but they threw us out. We left the lead in Oxhey Park on the way back to South Oxhey.

I was first through the door when we wandered into another part of the Crosse and Blackwell house. This section had been used as a doctor's surgery. I pushed open the door and was thrown right across the room after touching bare wires where the light fitting had been. We found a hypodermic needle and twelve morphine phials. I filled the needle with green ink and went about threatening to shoot kids full of it. Dick Herbert took it to Hampden School with similar intentions and the headmaster called the police.

'I found it on some waste ground, guv'nor,' said Dick Herbert.

No charges were made and I threw the morphine down a drain.

We all went to see *The Girl Can't Help It*, a film starring Jayne Mansfield and I was captivated forever by the frenzied performances of Little Richard Penniman in the film.

I had a home-made catapult with special leather swivel fittings, that had notches for streetlamps, notches for ceramic pylon insulators.

Tony Johnson was a big fat kid with a bow and arrow. He quite deliberately fired an arrow that hit me in the back. As he came up sneering, and bent down to pick up the arrow, I kneed him in the face. On the ground he was slow and inexperienced and was getting well beaten, so he fastened his teeth on my thumb. I wanted to kill him then, and held his nose until he opened his mouth and then put both my thumbs in his eyes. I was surprised at how hard his eyes were, I had expected a jelly like feel. I tried to crush them back into his skull. I couldn't stop myself, but he was much stronger, and broke free, picked up his bow and arrow and ran.

Richard Fordham left Hampden Secondary Modern and joined the Co-op as a trainee butcher. I started as a paperboy for Brooks, the newsagents and confectioners, at twelve and sixpence a week. Peter Naylor was told that he would be much happier at a secondary modern.

In the evenings we would often drift back to the recreation ground, it had no gates, fences or keeper, and just mess around. Sometimes, in summer, there would be a few other boys and girls, but usually it was deserted. Snooky Webster and a few of his mates turned up one night as we sat on the roundabout, just going round and round slowly, and talking. Now Snooky was about eighteen and had an enviable reputation, at that time he was probably the hardest and also the most jovial of the estate mob. We didn't know him to talk to, we'd seen him often enough, he lived just up the road.

'Right, you kids! Everybody off!'

And he was suddenly standing up there on top of the roundabout, grinning at his mates. We all jumped off fast, all except Richard Fordham that is, he was fifteen years old and big, but he was quiet and sensible, unlikely to ever start a fight.

'Didn't you hear me?' asked Snooky. 'Get off the bleeding roundabout!'

Richard just stood there. We all knew he would not get off.

'It's a free country,' said Richard. 'I don't see why I should get off, you don't own the thing.'

'Look mate, don't give me a lot of trouble. I don't want to sort you out, but you've got to get off now. Know what I mean?'

And his mates were waiting for it, they could not understand why Richard did not do as he'd been told. Then Snooky took off from the top of the roundabout, just threw himself head first at Fordham, crunching onto the tarmac and butting and punching like a complete madman.

He really enjoyed it, he was shouting and whooping all the time they were fighting. Richard was still in there with him, but wasn't getting many hits in. Snooky must have realized that he wasn't receiving any real damage himself.

'You had enough yet mate?'

'Well,' said Richard, steadily, 'I don't see why I can't go on the roundabout, just because you…'

Crunch! crunch!

And they were off again, but this time it was not long before Snooky stopped.

'Alright mate, that'll do. Good old go that was. You're a tough bastard alright.'

And he really meant it, was pleased that Richard had kept at it. He wandered away, unmarked and beaming, with his laughing mates.

Richard was in a right state, his face was a real mess, all lumpy, and bleeding in several places. It was while we were trying to work out how to sneak him past his parents that the policeman appeared. His arrival was just too much of a coincidence. Somebody from a house like mine, backing on to the recreation ground, must have called the police.

'Alright, lads, what's been going on here then?'

We were at the end of the alleyway leading away from the park, alongside Mrs. Bradstreet's house. We were standing in the shadows away from the streetlamp, trying to stand in front of Richard.

'Nothing constable, just mucking about, that's all.'

'Hey you! You at the back. Let's have a look at you.'

Richard Fordham slowly walked forwards.

'What's happened to your face?' Who's been knocking you about.'

'Nobody,' said Richard. 'I fell off the roundabout, didn't I.'

'Don't lie to me, son or you'll get another hiding. Who did it?

'Nobody did it, I fell off the roundabout. I've told you that already.'

Good old Richard, he really was a decent sort of bloke, by far the best of us in his kindness and lack of nastiness.

My sister got married in the June of 1957. Jim wore a charcoal drape suit, black crepe soled shoes and checkerboard socks. As it turned out, the wedding was a bit disappointing for Jean. The left side of her face had seized up some weeks before, and she could only move the right-hand corner of her mouth. It was all right as long as she did not attempt to smile, but the photographer couldn't help himself asking everybody to do exactly that. A few of the relatives cried later, when the rough proofs were passed around. Jim, at this point, had a year or so to do in the R.A.F. and they wanted to get the marriage allowance. To save for somewhere to live, Jean worked in a shop during the day and evenings in a cinema as an usherette.

We cycled to London Airport and they brought Dickie Herbert home in an ambulance. Younger than the rest of us, he had a lot of trouble keeping up. Exhausted by his efforts, he cycled head down straight into the back of a stationary lorry. We realised he'd fallen behind a bit and we'd stopped on the other side of the lorry, waiting for him to catch up. We saw him coming with his head down and knew he would not turn away in time. He did not hear us shouting, hit the back of the lorry and slid along the crossbar into the headstock. We were shaken by the screaming.

A caravan site at Dovercourt Bay with Mum and John, now five. Dad could not afford to take the time off work. I stood in the site amusement arcade, by the jukebox, with a Lonnie Donegan badge sewn onto my cotton zipper jacket, playing "Diana" by Paul Anka, until my money ran out.

Richard Fordham saved some of his wages and bought a transistor radio, but the only thing worth listening to was Radio Luxemburg, and that did not begin until seven o'clock in the evening. He also developed a special way of spitting through a gap in his teeth, combining great accuracy with a loud hissing noise.

The fair that summer was a good one. We paid two shillings and saw the boxing booth fighter hopelessly outclassed by a local amateur prospect called Bernie Murphy. The fight was stopped early and the fairground referee tried to call it a draw. It was obvious they'd stopped it early because their man was getting battered. There was a lot of booing and argument and the crowd disputed the shared purse, but eventually everybody wandered off. The striptease tent was exciting too, but they would turn the lights off as the girls got down to the last pieces of clothing. Some kids were said to have taken torches later in the week.

One Saturday we were hanging around the little humpy bridge near the cattle tunnel, Mick Goldsmith and Alan Fordham were building dam across the stream and I was carving my initials into a tree. Two older boys arrived, and with them were two girls that we knew, Rita Davenport and Pat Tucker.

The older boys asked us if we'd seen any boys from the Royal Masonic School, in Bushey. They were annoyed to hear that we had not, and explained that a fight had been arranged, to take place by the humpback bridge. The reason for the fight was also explained. A small group of Masonic kids had insulted Rita the week before, and as the honour of the Estate was involved a challenge had been issued and accepted. They had only just finished telling us this before the Masonic lot came marching through the cattle tunnel. At least thirty kids between sixteen and eighteen years old, some carrying sticks and all wearing the posh school uniform. They all stopped on the opposite side of the bridge and waited quietly whilst a runner was sent up to Taylor's café to fetch the reinforcements.

A good five minutes passed before they turned up. What an entry! I can still get excited about it, a whole army of madmen crashing through the bushes! They were carrying sticks, milk bottles from the café crate, and one kid was waving a sheath knife about, and one kid had an air rifle.

Brian Carter was big. He lived just around the corner from me and my mates but was a few years older and we didn't know him to speak to. They all stopped on our side of the bridge, Brian was in charge.

'Now then, Rita and Pat, is that right that these geezers said some bad things to you last week?'

'Yes, that's right Brian, they did,' said Pat, with a sidelong smile at the Masonic lot.'

'What did they say?'

And the girls giggling and looking at each other. About to speak, they cut short by Brian.

'I understand girls, you don't like to repeat it.'

And the way he said it, so sympathetic and so respectful.

'Anybody got a stick?' He looked over at us and then held his hand out.

'I'll have that, mate.'

Alan Fordham handed him the wooden fence post he had been using for the construction of the dam. It more than a metre long.

'Right, run you bastards!'

Total silence. Their leader was big but was wearing glasses. He stood his ground, clenching his fists and crouching down. Brian slowly brought the fence post back over his shoulder, a baseball player almost. Nobody else moved.

With a truly sickening thud, the fence post was swung full tilt into the side of the Masonic kid's head. I still don't know why he didn't stay down. One knee and one hand touched the floor and then he was up again. His broken glasses left on the ground.

'Somebody give me a stick.'

But it was no good. Nobody handed him a stick. He saw the fence post going back over Brian's shoulder, and ran.

The chase was on then, we threw everything at them in the stampede through the cattle tunnel, shouting and laughing, and the sharp click of the air rifle. They all escaped easily enough. The estate kids soon lost interest in the chase, it became more important to get back to Taylor's café and tell the tale.

Jim came home on leave and stayed in our house. He brought me a sheath knife from Germany, identical to the Hitler Youth model but with a fleur-de-lys on the hilt instead of a swastika. He also gave me a silver death's head ring he claimed was authentic Gestapo issue.

We all had track bikes, made with old frames and wheels found on the council dump. We used these for cycling over the golf course and in the local woods. Ordinary handlebars could be

bent to the angle of choice by jamming them into the iron
drainpipe of the house and pulling against them, and then
extended by jamming lengths of old gas piping into each end of
the handlebars. The aim was to imitate the speedway bike
handlebars that curved upwards and outwards. When a part of
my bike was worn out or broken, or I came across a better
component, I just threw the unwanted bits down into the
bottom of the First Dell, behind the house.
I took two wheels over one day and threw them over from the
highest rim of the dell. I was trying to hit a tree stump at the
bottom. I'd done this before, if a wheel hit the stump right it
would spring out of shape with a boinging noise. I even
scrambled down and fetched them up for another go if I missed.
After dinner the same day I was walking along the top of the dell
with Mickey Goldsmith, and I saw an old man right at the
bottom. He was sitting with one of my wheels beside him and
the other in his hands. He was holding it horizontally by the
spindle and spinning it slowly, sighting across the wheel to check
the distortion. The wheels were both wrecked beyond repair. He
did not notice me. He carefully put down the wheel and picked
up the other one, big patient hands turning it over. I could not
stand to watch any more - that poor old man - and hurried to
catch up with Mick. I said nothing to him in case he laughed.

Carl Stanhope and Geoff Keating had an automatic carbine rifle,
a 38 short-barrelled special, with shoulder holster, a full size 38
pistol, and several boxes of .303 blank ammunition, which for
some reason they thought might fit. They had stolen this
collection in a late-night raid on the U.S.A.F base behind our
school field. They went at night, on their bikes, during the
school holiday. Stanhope brought the large pistol to school. It
was so heavy I needed both hands to hold it. Stanhope's bike
had seventeen lights, all pinched from cycle racks in Watford.

The next fair arrived at Whitsun. I stood on the Tunnel of Love
walkway for hours, just to keep on hearing "Sweet Little
Sixteen" by Chuck Berry. I hung around with Dicky Barber as
they dismantled the rides on the last morning. He was older [at
least sixteen] and wore a drape suit with a long knife in his
waistband, suede shoes and silver dress rings. He'd arranged to
go off with the fair, sleeping in a locker beneath a generator

truck and washing out of a bucket. We went to Taylor's café to celebrate the decision.

Barbara Estep was really nice. Small and pretty, a gently spoken tomboy who asked nothing but that we be together. I stamped our initials on a penny using an alphabet die set that we had at home [It might have belonged to the my now departed Uncle Fred.] and then cut the penny in half with a hacksaw with a series of clumsy ziz-zag cuts. We were each to keep a section until the affair began to fade. The first one to send their half back to the other would officially end the relationship. We both kept the pieces of coin, but we somehow just drifted apart. We only met by being in the same place – near the recreation ground or near the café - nothing was arranged. We didn't have a telephone at home. If we saw each other that was good if not we did something else. I was always glad to see her, and she was always cheerful. Neither of us actually said we wanted to pack in in, we just lost touch.

Jim was demobbed and he and Jean found that they could not afford to buy a house after all. They went to live in a caravan at Waltham Cross, near Enfield. Three buses and two hours away from the South Oxhey Estate.

Our gang began a slow merger with Mac McFadden and his mates from the top end of Hayling Road, Tommy Quinn and Chris Howard. Mac was cheerful and very tough and Tommy had long blonde hair and could do handsprings. These were much rougher kids altogether, with the leather jackets and red baseball boots I couldn't afford.

The fair came back in July, and I was old enough to stay out later in the evenings. Long hot evenings and large crowds, and deafening music coming from the rides. The Teddy Boy fashion lingered late on the estate, and drape jackets were still to be seen. Studded belts were popular and I had a German military buckle on mine. [My Uncle George visited our house once and commented on the buckle. He'd been a prisoner of war in Germany in the First World War.]

The accident happened during the day, when the fair was not so crowded. We were all standing on the steps of The

Caterpillar and a girl fell out. She was about my age, taller than me, nice-looking. We had been watching her going round. Occasionally this sort of ride would have a cover come up over the customers, but mostly they didn't. The girl was in an outside seat and was having trouble hanging on to the handrail, laughing and screaming alternately. She came off as if in slow motion, just seemed to float out of the car. She came off at our exit, missed the upright, and travelled a good distance before landing on the grass. The woman who owned the fair was sent for [She lived on site in her caravan.] and when she arrived the girl began to talk to her. We were still on the steps and could see clearly, the girl was talking quite calmly but was not moving. I couldn't quite hear what she said. The woman told two fair workers to lift her up and see if she could walk. They stood her up. She couldn't walk, they had to let her down again and wait for the ambulance. I think she died before the ambulance arrived. It was in the papers. We thought it was the ride operator's fault, for running the Caterpillar too fast. The ride opened again two days later, but they ran it much slower this time.

Stephanie was young, attractive, and extremely good-natured. We got on well for a bit but that fizzled out, possibly because her friends were always with us. She was taller than me too.

I went to the Science Museum with Taff Evans. The stations were crowded with gangs of older kids heading for the Notting Hill race riot. It was rumoured to have started at a greengrocer's stall in Shepherd's Bush Market. We were going home, going the other way.

Barbara Roberts was a year older than I was. I went to her house every afternoon for a week. Her mother was at work during the day. She would put a stack of 78's on the radiogram, and we would be kissing on the settee under the window. It became very boring after an hour or two, but she had very fixed ideas about how we were to behave. I consulted Taff Evans for further advice, but it was a waste of time. Barbara was losing interest anyway, and other kids began to turn up on the doorstep.

The last week of the Summer Term at Bushey Grammar, and the traditional staff versus student cricket match. Nearly all the other pupils and most of the staff had gone home, but I remained in the corner of the field by the gym, down on the grass with Mavis Elliot. We were kissing now and then, but mainly just holding close together in the sadness of the long summer parting to come. And there was something wrong with the wicket, the staff were raising objections.

'Mavis!' shouted the new French teacher. 'Go and get the sawdust sack from the gym store.'

And she disengaged from me and began to walk over to the gym block.

'Boulter!' shouted Sid Caffall, the games master. 'Don't just sit there you lazy devil, go and help her carry it!'

Well, old Sid Caffall was all right, he had some faith in me. [He had put me in the school cross-country team and I took third place in the Southwest Herts Race at Rickmansworth. It was annoying, I missed out on second place to a kid who came up behind me right at the finish and clearly cut a corner without being penalised. It was also memorable for Robert Hine trying hard to get me to run with him all the way – telling me we'd get more points for the team if we came in together. I refused and he came in miles behind.] I set off after Mavis., we collected the sack, carried it between us and handed it over. They scattered it about on the wicket, and we took it back again. Neither of us thought much of it.

The next day we had French. The new man began by shouting at me about the state of my exercise book cover. [Now the cover was in a mess, but I had not drawn all the pictures myself.] Then he began raving about the cricket match incident and went crazy, calling me insolent when I naively reminded him that he had told Mavis to fetch the sack. It was just jealous rage, I knew it for certain, and so did Mavis, who was in the same class. At his best he was a miserable prematurely balding chinless awkward nuisance, and he had wanted to be on the grass with Mavis.

School was a dead loss. Sometimes I would take a whole week off, but usually just a day or two on alternate weeks. I was only ever caught once, and that was when I took an afternoon off, which was always a bit risky. The next day, Mr. Wilson the Math teacher asked me if I'd been off sick the previous day.

'No Sir.'

'Oh? Then why did you miss my lesson?'

'I was not at school Sir.'

'Oh. I suppose there was a golf tournament on, a bit of caddying perhaps?'

'No Sir, I just had to get away from school, Sir. I couldn't stand it any more.'

And he let me off completely, just told me to go and sit down again and get on with my work. Possibly he agreed with my motive. When I decided to hop school I always followed the same general plan. I would leave home as usual, in school uniform, with my lunch and a few odds and ends in my bag. At the bottom of my road I would cross over as if walking to the station, and then slip away down the alleyway leading to the woods. I had a regular hideout, a small clump of three or four pine trees in the exact middle of a large sloping cornfield, edged by thick woods on three sides. I would spend the whole day there, sitting with my back to one of the trees, keeping a low fire going even on warm days, using dry pines twigs to keep down the smoke. All I ever remember doing was smoking cigarettes and carving Indian heads or snakes at the end of sticks. I could hear the trains as they rattled past, high up on the embankment. They were beautiful days, the woods were mixed, an incredible variety of trees and plants, ferns, mosses, bright poppies in the cornfield, and a small stream running below the field. I loved to step from the bright daylit field into the cool dark woods, and try to see the green woodpeckers you could often hear but seldom saw. Dick Herbert would sometimes meet me in his dinner hour. He worked on Saturdays and after school, and did a few deliveries at lunchtime as well. After he had left I'd drift back into that primitive world again, dreaming against the pine. I had no fear of discovery, I could see all around and slip into the woods if challenged. I would go home for my tea. To eat and to change, to grumble about the imaginary school day and homework, and then go out again.

Café society beckoned and we slouched in, wearing Wescot jeans tapered by Mrs. Bradstreet for two shillings and sixpence. [Real trousers with turn-ups were three shillings and sixpence.] Our collars had to be just so – turned up at the back and down at the front. Smiling in any form was to be avoided. We stood around the Juke box and pintable in Bill Taylor's Café and listen to stories of sex and violence and great escapes.

> '…she was FOURTEEN I tell you!'

> '…really hit him, BROKE HIS BLOODY JAW!'

> '…came off an Ariel Square Four at NINETY!'

It was a confusing initiation into an expanding world of speed and excitement, even standing around was dangerous. Everything done for bravado, and for the story afterwards. Everybody wanted to be a star. Something was happening, we could all feel it, and sometimes hear it or see the signposts, but you couldn't explain it. Our world was tremendously exhilarating, and sometimes isolating. The language, the music, the clothes and the mannerisms were ours for a few precious years. If it was "just a stage" then it was one that our detractors would never pass through. Time seemed short, and if a girl was late you went without her, and vice versa.

I was fifteen on January the ninth, 1959, and wanted to leave school the same day. Dick Herbert was now the only other member of the gang who was still at school, and I was sick and tired of wearing a school blazer. But my parents were under the impression I had to stay at Bushey Grammar School until I was sixteen.

I went to Waltham Cross to visit my sister. She had asthma and was ill and in bed. I sat in a quiet café with my unemployed brother-in-law and played the Juke Box and drank tea very slowly. It was an old machine that still played 78's. I listened to Buddy Holly singing "I Guess It Doesn't Matter Any More." I remember the strangeness of this, as he'd died in an aeroplane crash 3 weeks earlier. I hadn't heard the song before and it was very different to his earlier upbeat songs, this one had melancholy lyrics about loss, separation, and departures.

Dick Herbert knocked for me one evening in April. I left him outside, went up to my bedroom and opened the window. I threw him down a bag containing a pullover, a sheath knife, twenty Senior Service and a box of Swan Vestas. Then we went off to meet up with the Fordhams and Taff Evans. [Dick Herbert posted my note through our letterbox on his way home again that night. "Goodbye, I've gone off to London."]

I broke into a kind of summerhouse, a posh tree house in the garden of Oxhey Grange, in Oxhey Lane near Watford Heath. I stayed up there until driven out by the cold at three in the morning. I then lay shivering in a ditch by the Community Centre as a policeman's torch flickered over the doors and windows. I then went to Carol Nesbit's bungalow, climbed over the back wall at four o'clock, and knocked on the bedroom window. Carol shared the room with her older sister. They wouldn't let me in until their parents had gone off to work. I rested on some neatly stacked paving slabs behind their garden shed, listening to pigeons in a loft behind me. I moved into the house and stayed with Carol until just before her parents came home again. I returned to her house again at seven o'clock to watch *Wagon Train* and wait for Alan Fordham and Dick Herbert, as previously arranged. They came with bad news. My mother was apparently going stark mad, and had been to all their houses and also told the police I was missing. The graphic and extremely gloomy descriptions of my mother's condition made me feel a bit guilty, so I decided to go home again. I persuaded Wendy Wallace to walk with me back to the house, as the boys did not want to be seen with me. They had denied all knowledge of my plan or whereabouts. I remember laughing with Wendy as we walked up Hayling Road, and kissing her outside the door.

'Oh well. Here we go. I'll see you tomorrow.'

My father took it fairly well, just threatened to hit me and then went off, muttering about having to inform the police.

My mother was upstairs, an incoherent stranger, totally child-like in her crying and saying the most pathetic things. Her appearance was unbelievable, hair all straggled down and big red eyes, her face swollen with crying. Making up my bed even as I tried to keep up with her, clinging to the sad domestic pattern. I could never think of much to say to my parents in normal circumstances, and putting my arm around her shoulder was not much use either, she just carried on making the bed. It was all a bit silly really, how could I comfort somebody that I wanted to get away from? And I still wanted to leave, nothing much had changed. I felt no sudden rush of tenderness and love when I saw my mother, I found her condition embarrassing. [This lack of concern was entirely unexplainable, both of my parents were, for the most part, kind, caring people who took care of all their children as best they could afford.]

After the failed running away caper my parents agreed to let me leave school. They also told Mr. Brooks he'd need to get another paper boy to replace me. This turned out to be annoying as I did not find a job for three months and could have done with the money. The last few weeks at school went very slowly. Only Wilson, the Mathematics teacher, tried to talk me out of leaving. I had usually played around during his lessons, so I was surprised when he made the effort. It was embarrassing for both of us, he tried to drop his formal schoolteacher manner and I tried hard to sound cheerful and respectful. The conversation was awkward, we were treading too carefully to really get anywhere, but at least we made an effort. A few of the girls showed some concern about my leaving, but my form teacher, who was also charged with teaching me Geography, was only worried about his stock, and his precious register.

'Now look here, Boulter, how long are you going to be with us? Is it worth you having a new exercise book?'

And I supposed that it was not really worth having a new book, although I did not know exactly when I was leaving. Before the end of term anyway.

A long white clubhouse, a paved terrace with an ornate stone parapet, wide steps leading down towards confident voices coming up from the green below, and the heavy sweet smell of cut grass. To the left of the clubhouse, the hut half-hidden in the ragged spinney. A hut of crumbling London brick, without windows.

The door was gone, there was no chimney, and the smoke from the brazier hung in the half-light before curling slowly up through the holes in the roof. Wooden beer crates around the oil drum table. Cement floor under layers of trodden ash and cinders. Blind Three-card Brag with Darkie and Staunch and Irish Mick, and many more without remembered names. Quarts of beer and medicine bottles, coughing shadows in corners, reaching without words to pick up the thrown ends of cigarettes. Waiting for the Caddy Master to shout a name, waiting for the pubs to open, or just waiting to go home. Two slogs around the eighteen holes at fifteen shillings a time, with only two call-outs from the Caddy Master in three months. Hiding out from employment, from the vacancy columns in the local paper, the 'experienced men only' and the 'minimum five 'O' levels.' Hiding from the new Youth Employment Exchange, with its Forestry Commission leaflets. Leaving the caddy hut at four, and dragging slowly back across the fields to the Estate, and the safety of Bill Taylor's café. Then going home, the mingling of hope and sadness in my mother's question,

'Did you go after anything today, Peter?'

KRISSON PRINTING WORKS

'Here you are son. It's just gone seven.'

Dad handing me the cup of tea. And going down to the dull fire in the front room, sieved cinders carefully relit from the night before. Sitting with my bowl of cornflakes resting on the arm of the settee, across from my father sitting next to the fire drinking his tea and smoking his Sun Valley roll-up.

'Off now, are you? You've got a good 5 minutes. Look after yourself.'

'Yeah. All right Dad, see you tonight.'

And the calling upstairs. 'Going now Mum'.

'Cheerio Pete, mind how you go love.'

Walking to the bottom of Hayling Road, turning right at Prestwick, and along to Carpenders Park Station, down the steps to the subway and up the slope to show the green season ticket and then on through to the platform.

Into the waiting room, chilly morning overcoat heavy with the motorbike carburettor and the bayonet I bought from Mazzoni. Looking for familiar names written on the yellow plaster walls, a hardboard sheet replacing the section of missing window glass.

Sitting in the corner of the carriage, to polish the carburetor with Duroglit wadding, then polishing the bayonet when the train began to empty out later. Ten stops, thirty minutes and two cigarettes to Harlesden, and the clattering feet crowding up the wooden steps to Acton Lane.

Over the bridge and past the cooling towers, past
Waxlow Road and the baked bean factory, past the green-tiled
pub on the canal bridge, and into the lorry dock at the back of
the works. Clocking in at four minutes past eight and losing
fifteen minutes pay out of the basic weekly wage of two pounds
fifteen shillings and sixpence. Into the locker room, with its
sleepy greetings, stripping down to underpants and t-shirt before
pulling on the boiler suit with the sleeves cut off above the
elbows.

And it's another day at Krisson Printing Limited and
I'm singing "Come Softly To Me" by The Fleetwoods
in the privacy of the oil store, staring out at the Velocette
Clubman with clip-on bars and rev-counter.

From tanks in the store, I re-fill the seven plastic
bottles with petrol, and another seven plastic bottles with some
kind of solvent, before pushing the trolley back into the machine
shop and replacing them in their racks beside each printing
machine. The men on the day shift are standing around, smoking
and talking with the outgoing night shift about the print runs in
progress. I crawl around at their feet with rags and a bucket,
mopping up the machine oil oozing over the floor. Some of the
grease is trodden down hard, and I scrape it up with a putty
knife. I hate this morning routine, the fumes from the petrol and
the solvent make me dizzy, and sometimes I have to sneak off to
the toilets and sit quietly for a bit with my head between my
knees, trying not to be sick.

Cleaning completed, I go over to my machine, a
Heidelberg Platen, and begin the over-printing of the Dexion
Slotted Angle Leaflets. Dexion is the parent company, and in the
spaces on the backs of their publicity leaflets I have to print the
names of stockists. My instructor is Tony, an older apprentice
working on an adjacent machine. No smoking after nine.
Watching as each leaflet is pulled into the machine, clonked by
the heavy platen containing the inked forme that contained the
letterpress type, and then dropped into the delivery tray. Trying
not to dream, trying to remember what I am supposed to be
doing, checking the leaflets in the delivery tray for quality of
print. Watching the clock high up over the dispatch bay, waiting
for the tea bell.

There is an unpaid evening class once a week, held in
the canteen, our attendance is expected. Talks are given by

various guest speakers, usually from the management side of Dexion. We are given copies of Henry Ford's biography and *How To Win Friends And Influence People* by Dale Carnegie. I received a Parker biro as the winning prize in the works' essay competition, but mine was the only entry. [As I edit this writing sixty-three years later, I'm aware that I have used Parker biros - in blue, black and red ink - ever since.] At the evening classes, as they listed the qualities required of top management, so I realized I did not have them. I scored high marks in countless tests of intelligence and aptitude, I successfully negotiated all the colour blindness testing books, and my file of work, with print samples and operating notes, was a masterpiece. I was mechanically-minded and had a fair knowledge of the wider aspects of the printing business. Having so carefully measured my ability, the management side and the machine shop foreman were puzzled by my somewhat erratic progress. Somehow they had failed to notice that I was a totally useless machine operator, that I could not concentrate upon a simple task for longer than twenty minutes at the most. They also failed to notice that I was bored to desperation, that my legs ached from standing up all day, and that all I wanted to do was go home. [I had problems with my legs when I was a child, apparently, although I do not remember it. My sister told me that my mother used to massage my legs to ease pain.]

Sandra Doyle had blonde hair and was really pretty, but could sometimes be a bit wilful, you needed to be careful not to upset her. I paid her fare to Cassiobury Park once, to the wooded slope overlooking the canal, looking down on the Sunday boats leaving the lock. We lay together, just talking and kissing for at least an hour. Then Sandra sat up and began combing her hair, telling me it was time to go back.

I had picked a really stupid place to work. It was the school in the wrong place business all over again. All my mates worked in Watford, came home for dinner or ate in famous local cafes. They were not remotely interested in my job in Acton. This workday isolation did nothing to improve my venomous personality. On more than one occasion – in broad daylight, coming home from work – I would confront young men of my own age or thereabouts.

'You staring at me mate?'

'What? Nah, course I ain't.'

'Want a smack in the mouth?'

And yet such ridiculous behaviour seemed not
unreasonable at the time, among my own crowd.

Home again. Hello to Mum and Dad, acknowledge brother
John, stroke the cat curled against the spark guard on the hearth,
and say hello to Trixie our ancient dog. Fried egg all whisked up
as I liked it, baked beans, bacon, fried potato and Worcester
Sauce. Cup of tea. Upstairs to get changed.
　　　　Tight black cords with James Dean medallion, made in
Belgium, hooped cotton socks from Portugal, black fire-
damaged suede boots from Petticoat Lane. Black shirt with gold
lurex on the front and collar, made in Hong Kong, and a dark
blue cotton zipper jacket. Door key on a leather bootlace around
my neck, a clean Woolworth's snuff handkerchief in the front
trouser pocket and money in the left.

'Off now then, Mum. See you later Dad.'

'All right Peter, going anywhere special?'

'No, just round to see the boys, might go to the
pictures later.'

'See you then.'

And out. Run up the four steps and through the gateway,
straight over the road to Dick Herbert's house opposite. Dick
comes out of the door backwards, edging through it as he closes
it, shouting back into the house, competing with the row coming
from the television. Once out, he turns and leans on me, and we
push and shove each other down the front path. Turn right out
of the gate and past the new kid's house, a ginger-haired kid too
young to hang around with us. He has twin brothers of twelve or
thirteen, kids with muscular dystrophy who have to be carried

out to a special school bus each day, sweet-smiling in the driver's strong arms, their legs swinging with his every step. And then it's only two minutes before we arrive at the Fordham house. Alan slams the door and grins at us.

'Arghh! It's Wimpy!' Screams Dick Herbert, mock-vomiting over the hedge outside the house.

'Wotcha Al, how's things?' I say. 'Cut off anybody's ears lately?'

And Al pretends to make a run at us and we scramble back to the pavement.

'What about Richard?'

'He's not coming, his throat's bad. He's got to stay in.'

'Are we knocking for Pricey?'

'What for?' We don't want him with us.'

'Course we ain't, he won't come out anyway.'

'Well come on then, let's get round to Taff's.'

And it's a few steps to get round the corner and up through the trees in Birkdale Gardens, across Fairfield Avenue and down the alley to Taff's back door. Then into the kitchen and talking to Mr. Evans whilst Taff gets ready upstairs. Waiting out on the grass verge for Dave Harrison to turn up on his Claude Butler, then waiting whilst he puts the bike in Taff's shed, then all drifting off to Taylor's Café.

It was the summer of fifty-nine, and only Dick Herbert was still at school. Alan Fordham was working in a local hairdresser's shop and had picked up the name of Wimpy due to Dick Herbert claiming he resembled a character in the television cartoon *Popeye the Sailorman*. Eventually the nickname Wimpy went away and he went back to being Alan, or Al. His brother Richard was still training as a butcher, but had developed some kind of throat trouble, and had recently been in hospital for tests. Pricey worked in a warehouse, and was as moody as ever.

Taff was an apprentice machine operator in a printing works in North Watford, and was now firmly established as our social organizer. Whenever he was missing we tended to argue amongst ourselves, and could never think of anything interesting to do. Dave Harrison had been in the same class at Hampden School as Taff and Pricey, and had a job on a farm just outside Watford. He was almost pretty and lived on the Carpenders Park Estate. but he seemed all right and got on with everybody. We also mixed frequently with MacFadden's lot from the top of Hayling Road, but our meetings were seldom organized. Usually we met them on neutral ground, at clubs, or at the Sunday night horror films in Watford.

Bill Taylor's cafe was always our starting point. From there, under Taff's direction, we would set off on a tour of the estate, looking for girls. The sort of girls we came across would generally be hanging about near their own homes, and always had to go indoors early. But we could often make arrangements to meet them at the weekend, when they were allowed more freedom. The best girls with those we met in the shopping area, or at the recreation ground, the girls who could stay out late or didn't care if they did. The rec was a problem, as it was very near my house in the evenings were still fairly light. I always had to keep my voice down.

Adam Chadwick had a party at his house, when his parents went out one evening to visit relatives. It wasn't much of a party, just our lot, McFadden's bunch, some bottles of beer. There were three girls, Sandra, Rosie, and Sheila. The beer spilling incident wrecked any chance we might have had with any of them. It was Wimpy's fault, he was messing about and knocked a cup of brown ale over Sandra's pink taffeta dress. She'd thought it was going to be a real party, with music and dancing. She was too frightened to go home with a stain on the dress, so she sponged it down and then took it off to iron it. The girls locked themselves in the kitchen to do this, but were unfamiliar with the layout of the house. They had locked the door from the kitchen to the hallway, but had not noticed another, unlocked door leading from the kitchen to the front room. This was easy to miss as the back of the door was covered with coats. Chadwick hogged the keyhole first, as she took the dress off, and then we began quietly to ease the door open. Now another thing that the girls did not know about was the state of Chadwick's father, who only had one arm. They were facing the locked door to the hall, arguing with Wimpy on the other side, when Sandra first felt Chadwick's father's spare arm slipping coldly between her legs. Screaming, she jumped away from the alloy fingers and spun round, to see the plastic forearm and the shiny steel elbow joint and to see the leering Chadwick on the other end.

Warren Lewis was a bit different. We all knew him because he lived near the shops and was in Wimpy's class at Hampden. He was pale, wore glasses and a and wore sports jackets and baggy trousers. He was known for mucking about with old radios and making models, and was seldom seen out and about. But his popularity shot up when his parents went on holiday for a week and left him behind. Left with the house to himself for a week, Warren was overjoyed to find that we all liked him a lot, and that we all greatly admired his model making skills. We waited at the end of the road until the car had collected his parents, and then went to the house. The party carried on for the full week and got better every night, with lots of boys and girls we didn't know turning up. The neighbours called the police twice and we left Warren on the last night with two hours to repair the place before his parents came home. We took quarts of cider and half bottles of Australian sherry, and Wimpy optimistically provided prophylactics from the barbershop. Pricey supplied the records and the Dansette record player.

Towards the end of the party week I was fetched from the landing toilet by Mac, and pulled back into the bedroom where I had just left Rosie. Colin Stanton stood by the window, and Rosie was still on the bed. It appeared that, during my absence from the room, Colin had wandered in, attempted to perform with Rosie and failed completely. He was two years older than me and had lost a lot of respect. Understandably annoyed, he had turned to McFadden for ideas. They wanted me to repeat the act as a kind of practical demonstration for Colin. Rosie and Mac were laughing, and the drink had now caught up with me so we all went back to the chaos downstairs instead.

On the last day of the party, I arrived to find two boys holding a fully dressed Rosie in the bath, while Pricey turned the taps on. I turned the taps off again and hit Pricey on the knee with a pint bottle, then punched him in the face as he doubled over. Rosie was one of us, a friend, and not to be treated badly.

With the last summer of the nineteen fifties long gone, and Autumn arriving, so Wednesday nights at St. Martin's Youth Club became important again. St. Martins Church Hall was a new building with plenty of big windows, and the Vicar only stayed from seven to seven-thirty, then reappeared at ten to chuck everybody out. Anybody could go there but you did have to sign in.

It was probably the best place to meet girls, and the music was loud enough. We would arrive at eight o'clock, go straight to the toilets to comb our hair, then up onto the stage. This was the best place. You could watch both the door and the girls dancing at the other end of the hall. I have no memory of any of us dancing with any of the girls but it was a good place to fool around, play table tennis and meet both boys and girls from other parts of the estate.

John Kavanagh was still at Bushey Grammar, and he used to go to the St. Martin's club as well. One evening he arrived with a letter from Mavis Elliott. I was sitting back to front on a church chair, tilting it back on two legs. I waved the letter at the other boys.

'Look at this, it's a letter from a girl I know.'

'You lying bastard, you wrote it yourself I expect.'

'She really fancies me, don't she?

It was a letter written on pages torn from an exercise book, and I found it a sad and desperate. A short letter, from 'Hello Pete, how are you getting on?' to a few mentions of people and events at the school, her unhappiness at being at the Cally, and her last words.

'I miss you, Pete, I love you. When can I see you again?

I was upset by it, but knew better than to show it. I had a job I didn't want, and a girlfriend I could not reach. I convinced myself I had the nerve to go to the fearsome

Caledonian School, over the imaginary perimeter wire, but also knew they would really fix Mavis if I was caught doing it. All I could manage was to write on the back of her sad pages, to shut out the club record player and the boys nudging and jeering, and try to put my love on lined paper. I gave my reply to Kavanagh to take back.

The year was nearly gone. It was just a few days before Christmas, and Chadwick's dad was standing at the Hayling Road bus stop, in his heavy winter coat. And two kids were asking him the time. The watch was hanging at his left side, strapped around the worn brown gauntlet on his wrist. He lifted his left wrist with his right hand and turned it, in order to see the face of the watch.

Click! Click! Click!

'Well, lads, its eleven o'clock, but I might be a bit fast.'

It was Easter 1960, I was now sixteen, and Kevin Sinclair's dad wouldn't be needing the Hillman. Rather than cause him extra worry, Kevin didn't bother to tell him we would be taking it to the South Coast. It was easy really, Kevin been using the car since he was sixteen, when his father first went into the hospital. He was now seventeen but had never taken a test and was not insured either. He'd had keys cut for both the garage and the car, no sense in it rotting away in the garage. It was a decent car, you could get Luxembourg on the radio and it had bench seats so you could get six people in it. It was unlikely that Kevin's dad would ever drive it again. We first went over to Bushey to pick up the others. Things were bit disjointed on the estate, and it was not always possible to assemble the people you wanted all at the same time, especially when we planned to be gone for several days. We took whoever we could find. Ray Parker and Morton Smith both had essential qualifications. Morton had a full license, and Parker had some money to help pay for the petrol. John Angus also came, and we already knew him and liked him. He was big and tough, and looked much older than he was. He also knew people on the coast. We left at midnight, as Kevin couldn't drive so well with other cars about.

We drove to Poole Harbour, where John Angus renewed a holiday relationship. The girl brought along two friends, and we drove inland to swim in a river. Now these girls were young, but very strong and fit. Strong swimmers, they changed behind bushes and jumped straight into the clear water. It was getting on for one and a half metres deep in some sections, and running very fast over a shingle bottom. Kevin had swimming trunks and was a very powerful swimmer, John was up on the bank with his girl, Morton was hanging about the car, and Ray had gone off for a walk. Kevin joined the two girls in the river and I thought I ought to get in myself.

I was a very poor swimmer, and didn't have any trunks, but an impression had to be made. Now it was one of the annoyances of those times that you could not get the clothes you wanted, you had to buy the existing stuff and get it altered. I was wearing a pair of standard thick green corduroy trousers tapered down by Mrs. Bradstreet to thirty centimetre bottoms. This was fine, but she would not attempt to alter waistbands, that was too complicated. The waistband was far too big for me and the trousers were held up by braces. Having removed all my clothes except for the trousers and braces, I jumped into the river, It was a big mistake. The current filled up my trousers and the water could not escape fast enough from the tight bottoms. In seconds I was transformed into a curly-haired green cone hurtling feet first downstream at about thirty miles an hour. That blew it with the girls, they saw me as a complete twerp, and fell about laughing. But I was actually in dead trouble, I couldn't stop. Luckily, the force of the current threw me up onto a shingle bank on an outer bend in the river and I was able to crawl up the bank unaided, to slink gloomily back to the motor.

Damp and excited, with a new passenger, John's girlfriend, we arrived at Beaulieu. We were totally unprepared for the scene that met us, and the unimaginable excitement. A village of youth and madmen. Freaks everywhere, playing guitars, banjos, even trumpets and a slide trombone, drinking from gallon jars of cider, wearing animal skins and sacking, wide-eyed and joyous. It was as if the whole youth culture had found a temporary home, a place to strengthen the group identity. We had never been particularly interested in jazz, but the times were changing, and we knew some of the bands. The people crowding the street actually cheered us in, me and Kevin from off the South Oxhey Estate!

And it was the right year to be there, the year of the television cameras and the television tower - the year of the Beaulieu riot. Ambulances and police cars running shuttles to the hospital and the nick, and no less than five fire engines! It was the first time I was to experience crowd panic. Those of us in front of the stage - a converted fairground roundabout - were standing up, and the crowd behind us got nasty because they couldn't see. They then threw cans and bottles towards the front.

Suddenly, everybody seemed to go crazy and there was a mass press towards the stage. We could only go forwards towards the band. I climbed up on the stage and stood next to Shirley Duncan, the singer in the Clyde Valley Stompers, and she was as scared as I was. Kevin got up and in the way of the bass player, who was running across the stage holding his bass as a shield. He caught Kevin on the head with the shoulder of the bass and he was knocked straight out. The piano was pushed over the edge and just fell to pieces. People on the floor were reaching up and trying to grab me, to pull themselves up to safety. Somebody hit me and I swung a chair at them, another chair hit me and I was knocked off the back edge of the stage. I fell a short distance and landed on a pile of spare chairs, escaping with a lightly sprained wrist and a few cuts. I managed to get to Kevin, who was now on his feet and stumbling about the stage, and we started to walk back to our tent. Then the television tower went down, and the ambulances and fire engines began to wail through the park. We went back to a night of drinking and trying to sleep, listening to the guitars and bongos in the tent next door. The next evening was different. The Acker Bilk Band arrived on a Stagecoach and his calm voice and jovial music calmed everybody down for a gentle ending.

A SAD RETURN

Back home, Bushey Grammar School had a new sports pavilion, and held a special open day to show it off to the parents. It was held on Saturday, and as an old boy of the school, I felt it necessary to attend. I managed to interest of fair number of people in the trip, including Jimmy Knight, hod carrier and ex-pupil a year older than myself.

About twenty of us set off, with Dave Harrison and Chrissy Howard pledged to arrive later on their motorbikes. I made an effort to be tidy, and wore a new jacket – one of the short Italian jackets that were coming in on the Estate. I was excited and edgy, remembering my failures at the school. It didn't occur to me to blame myself of course. We went by train to Bushey Station and then walked to the school. On the way, Jimmy pulled down a section of the Masonic School fence, went into the grounds and picked up a rugby ball and threatened one of their pupils before throwing it back.

It was a really hot day, and when we got to Bushey Grammar, it seemed most of the parents had stayed away, and there were hardly any children of school age either. We didn't have to do anything to be annoying, we just wandered about. We looked at the new pavilion and Mr. Smith, the deputy head, in a roundabout way, asked me if I had the keys. He was in a right state. He was very red in the face, and awkward, nothing like the authority of the year before, the man who had kept my year behind after assembly and told us forcefully, that there was no doubt about it.

'THERE MUST BE A GOD!'

He seemed unsure how to approach me. My first name he had probably never known, and it was obviously a bad move to call me by my surname, and to use the Mister prefix was also not an option. He finally got around it carefully, presenting the problem first, explaining to us that the pavilion had been locked and the keys were missing, therefore the parents couldn't get in to look around. Since we had just come from there - they'd had a good look around obviously – but they must find them soon.

And I told him I hadn't seen them, which was true. I can't vouch the others, but none of them ever admitted it later. Mr. Smith was stuck. He believed I'd taken the keys but there was not much he could do about it. I was outside his jurisdiction. I was small and thin, and presented no threat but I was obviously enjoying his discomfort, and he couldn't risk rolling in the dirt with a sixteen-year-old. It was unthinkable. He finally suggested that I'd had my little joke, and that if the keys were found he would forget about the incident. But if not he would have to call the police.

I told him I didn't have the keys and walked away. I wanted him to call the police to his sunny domain, to see helmets among the few floppy hats of the ladies. One parent did crack, however, and started to push one of the boys about, and kept telling him to apologise the swearing in front of his wife and kids. We all stood around them in a circle and waited. The estate kid stood his ground just holding the man off when he tried to push him again. The man was really shouting at one stage, but finally he had to walk away. There was nothing he could do, he had been made to look foolish certainly, but it would've been far worse if he had actually struck out. His failure discouraged the rest of the parents.

Chrissy and Dave arrived and revved up. The police turned up shortly after. They'd been called by the Masonic School, not Mr. Smith, and the kids there had simply pointed up the road to where we'd gone.

I was leaning up against a wall as the police arrived. It was near the exit gate. A woman began to scream at the police.

'He's the one! He's the ringleader. Over here officer. Quickly! Over here, there is! There! There! That's the one!'

And she was jumping up and down and pointing at me. The police rushed over and then found that I had done nothing, I just didn't look so good. We denied breaking the fence, stealing the ball, and stealing the keys. They just told us to shove off back to South Oxhey and we left.

The walk back to the station was for me a disappointment. I tried to run over the events with the rest of them, but I wasn't really up to it. At the school I had been called over to the Caledonian fence by Ann Coulter, a friend of Mavis Elliott and a fellow resident. She was standing on their side of the fence. She had left Bushey Grammar and was now a nurse to the infants playing at her feet. To stay at the Cally she now had to earn her keep. She was excited to see me but could only speak for a few minutes before taking the children back inside. Mavis had gone. Ann believed she'd tried run off and been caught, and had subsequently been sent away to somewhere near Plymouth, to live with a relative.

'I'm sorry Pete, but I didn't see her again after she ran away, so I don't know the address. She said she'd write.'

Barry was eighteen, a fellow apprentice. Big and very strong, he had five O-levels and was very annoying. He had decided that I was visually and generally objectionable, and that being the newest and smallest arrival I could be picked on. He said that I was cheeky, and whenever he passed by me he would hit me on the shins or elbows with a typescale, a metal printer's ruler about thirty centimetres long. Now this really hurt, and was itself worthy of retaliation , but there was also verbal accompaniment.

'Think you're tough don't you? You little squirt.'

A whack with the typescale.

'Don't be cheeky laddie!'

Another whack with the typescale, followed by a high girlish giggle.

I told him to stop it, and began the necessary ritual prior to retaliation. I told him to stop it again and again, before witnesses. I shouted it in the works canteen and on the shop floor, made sure everybody knew the situation. I kept it up for two weeks, never attempting to avoid the hits, never attempting to retaliate or run away. I was almost enjoying it, knowing that I would sort him out eventually, once I had covered myself with the other men. Barry certainly enjoyed himself, and said I was a scrawny little coward who was only brave in a gang. He expected fear. Expecting to see it, he imagined he saw it.

In the course of the job, we used little modelling knives rather like fountain pens, but with adjustable blades instead of a nib. I set mine to protude one centimetre and then asked Barry to show me his birthday wristwatch. As he held out his bare arm, I gripped his fingers and then cut the underside of his arm from elbow to wrist. with the knife I'd hidden at my side. He was very surprised. He did not cry out. It was all too sudden. He just jerked away and stared at his arm. He saw the red line, filling over at the edges and running down his arm, turned very pale and began to tremble. He recovered very quickly and rushed away, to get himself patched up. It was only a very deep scratch and was soon plastered over. He said he would tell the foreman, which was what I had expected. He also threatened to beat me up after work, which I was not so happy about. I told him that if he tried I would kill him.

At four o'clock, the end of the day shift, it was quiet in the locker room. All the men were getting out of their overalls and getting dressed to go home, but slowly. Barry had been telling everybody all afternoon what he was going to do to me. I was not afraid. Tense and excited, yes, but not afraid. I was half dressed and my jacket was hanging beside me on the locker door. In the side pocket was my Spanish lock knife with the blade opened earlier. Barry been waiting all afternoon to get me but I'd been planning for two weeks to fix Barry.

'Got you now, you little rat!'

And the men stopped dressing as Barry came in, smacking the flat side of his typescale against his palm and then coming up to me and prodding me gently with it. But I could see he wouldn't hit me, could see in his face that he just didn't have the stomach for it. He tried some sneering remarks about bravery with knives, cowardice and being unable to take a joke, and looked around at the older men for support. Some of the men chipped in, calling me a mad sod and suchlike, appearing to side with Barry in condemning my actions. But I saw approval behind their grins, got dressed and went happily home. There was no more bullying.

Despite hating the job, I got on well with most of the men at the printing works. They were a mixed bunch. Dave was trying to avoid being called up for National Service by going to a doctor regularly to fake a back problem. When he finally had his call-up medical they turned him down anyway because he had flat feet.

We had three ex-Royal Marines in that small place and when I asked one of them what he thought about killing people, he told me he didn't know. He said he just ran about dodging and shooting. Some of the people he shot at might occasionally fall over but he couldn't be sure he'd killed them. My instructor on the Litho machine, Mervyn Taylor, had a Bond Minicar with just one wheel at the front. He dropped me off in Central London a couple of times as he lived right across on the other side of the city. The compositor who owned the Velocette Clubman once dropped me off at a big motorcycle dealer in Brixton. A truly terrifying ride in the London rush hour.

That summer, I went away for a holiday by the sea, just me and Dave Harrison, with lots of decent clothes and a stack of town guides listing bed and breakfast places. We caught the milk train from London Bridge station and stumbled out at Hastings, putting our suitcases in the left luggage room. We hung around the town on the beach all day and managed to creep into a packed pub later on. This was the first time I ever saw anybody playing a resonator guitar, a wooden archtop with a metal resonator set in the top of the body. In the pub we met up with two older boys from Rochester, who knew of a late-night jazz dance being held in a local park. We all drifted along and spent a couple of hours of dancing and fooling about before going back to the front to find a place to sleep. There were about fifteen others by then, and we felt very excited and adventurous. We stayed, finally, under a huge pile of deckchairs in Bottle Alley, singing and telling stories nearly all night.

This carefree beginning shaped the rest of the holiday and afterwards we could never be bothered, or were more likely too nervous, to knock on the doors of seaside landladies. We left our stuff at the station, and just wandered about for a week. We walked from Hastings to Worthing and back, via Eastbourne and Brighton. We walked mostly in the early mornings, or at night, sometimes along the coast roads and sometimes across country high up over the South Downs. We slept in an empty car, an empty shop, an upturned dinghy, and a roadman's hut. Once, at daybreak we awoke in one of the caves at Hastings, twenty metres above the beach. It was cold, and we sat in the cave mouth drinking Mateus Rosé and smoking Rubicon mixture in my ten shilling cherrywood pipe. Not talking, just staring out at the choppy sea, watching the seabirds swoop and caw over the deserted coastline. I'm not even sure that we enjoyed the holiday, sometimes it was as if we only kept going for the sake of the story afterwards. We were sleeping in our summer clothes, we hadn't taken blankets or raincoats and most of the week we were very cold and wet, and it was never hot enough during the day to get properly dried out.

The police took us from a club in Eastbourne, and questioned us for two hours before telling us to go home. [Dave was wearing a milkman's hat and they'd matched him to a description of a wanted seaman, or so they said.] We were just stepping onto the beach at Brighton when we were picked up again. This time it was me, I was thought to be a runaway from the Borstal at Portland Bill. They rang Dave's parents and let us go, and again we were told to go home. Finally, limping back into Hastings at six in the morning, we were pulled into a patrol car. They checked with headquarters on the radio and then let us out. That time we were going home anyway, we had run out of money and our feet hurt.

Perhaps the most significant thing about the holiday was that I had gone with Dave, that the others had stayed behind. Things were changing on the estate as we became older, and legally entitled to steer dangerous machinery. Soon nearly all of us had motorbikes or cars. I didn't have any savings and didn't earn much. My ex-WD Royal Enfield, a 350cc with scrambles bars and alloy guards, was a disgrace. Richard Fordham and Tommy Quinn both had cars. If your bike wouldn't go, if you missed a lift in a car, you either had to stay indoors or get round to the café to see if anything else was happening that you could latch onto. The old gangs began to break up as a result, and new stars appeared, often previously useless kids who had somehow managed to buy a Triumph Bonneville or Austin Atlantic.

Everybody began to move further away from the Estate at night, going to clubs in Rickmansworth, Watford, Chesham and St. Albans.

Taff and Dick Herbert were busy riding about on Taff's BSA Star. Dave was in hospital with broken ankle after crashing his motorbike into a fence. Richard was in hospital again with throat trouble, and Kevin's dad was dead. Kevin kept his shaving mug and wedding ring and tried to keep the payments going on the Hillman. Kevin also had a steady girlfriend and was on probation.

Mum got a job at British Home Stores in Watford and met "a nice quiet girl" there.

'She says she knows you, Peter.'

And it was Rosie, doing a Saturday job.

I took Vivian Henderson on the Tunnel of Love when the fair arrived again. During the ride she clung onto the safety rail. We said goodbye afterwards and I slipped away into the crowd. I had always got on with her at school, and thought a lot of her, would have liked to move things on. There was definitely a connection, but she was still taller than me and that was enough to spoil everything at that time.

The lady across the road took her smiling sons to Lourdes. I can't remember how that turned out.

I met a girl who was only a few months older than me but seemed much older. She bit me once, and hard, for no reason I could think of. She wore quite a lot of makeup, which was unusual then, and we often wrestled in the cow field by the lakes. But she was too heavy, and too soft to the touch. It was an odd thing I'd discovered when dancing, that with some girls the touch of hands was too soft, too passive. This was a strange reaction, but little things seemed important to me then...soft bits were important obviously, but not an overall softness. Clammy hands, limp hands and being too quiet was wrong, and cackling or nervous behaviour also seemed wrong, but I cannot recall any of these dislikes were ever mentioned or discussed with my friends at the time. Physical and verbal resistance and argument was expected, any relationship worth having was assumed to involve ongoing struggles and adjustments. Maybe some of the other people were looking for more docile partners.

Everything seemed to be both picking up speed and falling to pieces. I began to see excitement in all directions, stretching far beyond the South Oxhey Estate, but I also needed stability. I needed the gang most when it all began to fall apart.

Krisson Printing I didn't need. I gave notice in the morning and walked out after lunch. I walked slowly down Acton Lane, carrying both boiler suits. There were plenty of backward glances too, I wanted to remember it all clearly, it was a racing certainty that I wouldn't ever be going back.

DAYS OF WONDER

Ronnie Hopwood was out. We were sitting in a Watford café, admiring his tattoos and rolling cigarettes with his special fag papers, stamped 'HM Prisons.' Ronnie was a bit different. He had a dishonourable discharge from the army, and had spent months in military prisons in Cyprus and England, and done a nine-month stretch in Brixton for car theft and resisting arrest. He was tall and good-looking and liked good clothes, a sharp dresser with a gentle voice. A few years older, he was challenging company. Anxious to please, he would crush beer glasses in his hands and stub cigarettes out on his knuckles. I once saw him punch a horse in the head, without any warning, just because he thought it would amuse us. All he wanted to do was to get back into the army, he even signed on using his brother's name, but was discovered and thrown out again. Chrissy Howard was with us too, just about the only one left from McFadden's lot. Mac himself was in the army. Tommy Quinn was found to have a weak heart. He found an easy job in an office and stayed in every night so as not to get too excited. Chrissy was a housepainter, but Ronnie and I were both out of work.

From the café we went to a pub opposite, and from the pub, at my persuasion, we went next door to the jazz club. The Watford Jazz Club was held every Thursday night in the Ex-Servicemen's Club function room, admission price only four shillings. A small side hall of brick and asbestos, hot and crowded, with condensation streaming down the walls.

She was wearing blue jeans and a torn shirt without a collar. Her father's shirt I was told later. She had short red hair, was dancing in bare feet, had pale blue eyes and was wearing a CND badge. She was a girl I knew slightly from Bushey Grammar, a girl I'd once danced with briefly at the old Essoldo Cinema, at their Saturday lunch hour sessions. She was dancing now with Micky Reiss. Ronnie and Chris were never going to dance, so as the band finished the tune I left them and pushed through to the girl. Blocking out Reiss, I grabbed the girl's hand as the band began playing "Tiger Rag." We stayed together until the club closed and walked together to her bus stop. We arranged to meet again.

Alison Barraclough. No middle name. A year younger, about three centimeres shorter, and a stone lighter. Short-sighted and intelligent enough not to wear glasses. Sullen in repose and vicious in her sudden anger. To me it seemed a perfect match but she was not so sure. I had fancied her when I was at school. She was not nearly so keen on me, and it required a special effort on my part to improve the situation. We went to London, to the Studio 51 Club, the 100 Club, and the Marquee. We sat around in Le Macabre, Le Partisan, Heaven and Hell, and The Nucleus. I showed her the delights of Petticoat Lane and Brick Lane and the Portobello Road and Shepherd's Bush Market. It was not until the fourth week, sitting drunk on the long seat near the door, on a red bus back from seeing a band in Harrow, that she first said she loved me. From there on things began to pick up.

I was working again and reading again. I was a laboratory assistant in a scrap metal yard attached to Watford Foundry, and was spending most of my lunch hour in the North Watford Public Library next to the St. Albans's Road roundabout. This was ten minutes away if I went through a section of the fence alongside the bypass. I was interested in communism at the time. I'd read *The Communist Technique in Great Britain* by Bob Darke, and was looking for *I Believed* by Douglas Hyde. This second book had been suggested to me by Mr. Ford, the chemist I was working with. He wanted to steer me away from the CP. I knew it, but I had a lot of respect for him, and he certainly helped me to think more about things. I found the Hyde book, but also picked up another book on the shelves close by, simply attracted by the peculiar title, *The Dharma Bums.* I had accidentally discovered Jack Kerouac. I read the book that evening and was back the next day to pick up *On The Road* and *The Subterraneans.*'

I began to spend more and more time with Alison. I would often stay at her house on Saturday nights, after arriving back late with her from London. I slept on the living room floor. I would wake up on Sunday to the rattle of the ashpan in the coal-fired room heater, as her father cleared the night's ashes and put on more fuel. He very rarely spoke, but would sometimes smile and say good morning if I managed to get up before he set off to church.

Alison's parents were both from Northumberland, and by education and profession they were what I then identified as middle class. They seemed totally unaware of my carefully cultivated nastiness. I would arrive with my shirt collar turned up, with my authentic Gestapo ring and chewed fingernails. Her mother would serve me with lemon tea from an alloy pot, and pass homemade cakes from a trolley. At first I found it confusing, and could not understand where I had gone wrong, but I learned to enjoy it, to look forward to talking to the mother, and being listened to.

There were almost too many things to do together, and work and school respectively became frustratingly long periods of dead time, interruptions to our racing relationship. To the Watford Beat Club on Wednesdays, and the Watford Jazz Club on Thursdays. Every Saturday we would go out for the day, usually to London but sometimes getting rover tickets on Green Line coaches. We went to Richmond and Kew, Hampstead and Chelsea, St Albans, and Wapping and Limehouse. And always with the green duffel bag, a packet of Lucky Strikes, and the secondhand Kodak Brownie. And for Christmas a gallon jug of cider and Ruffino Chianti from Parmigianni's in Old Compton Street. From Alison, the City Lights edition of Kerouac's *Book of Dreams*, hot from Zwemmer's import box in their Charing Cross Road bookshop.

January 1961 was cold, and had begun with contractors fencing off part of the golf course and the Third Dell. It was beginning to freeze again that Sunday afternoon when Alison and I caught the bus to Watford. We walked down Rickmansworth Road to the park gates, the original gateway to Cassiobury Park. Walking through the middle of the quiet park, past the shuttered tea room, the deserted bandstand, and the empty paddling pool.

It was early in the year for the floods, but the river was high enough then as we stepped carefully along the old wooden bridge to the island. As we reached the end of the path we saw that the river had already covered part of the island. It would never cover it completely, as the centre of the island and the land around the bridge supports had been raised many years before. A single tree stood on the lower ground, the shallow floodwaters pulsing through exposed roots with each surge of the heavy water. A twisted willow, its empty branches stretching down towards the rotting logs beneath.

'Alison?'

And she turned back to face me, black stockings and her mother's St. Hild's college scarf.

'Will you marry me?'